SEIZE THE MEANING!

Help Your Child Move from

Learning to Read to **Reading to Learn**

BY

PRISCILLA L. VAIL, M.A.T.

Adapted for parents from
Reading Comprehension: Students' Needs & Teachers' Tools

SIMON & SCHUSTER
New York London Toronto Sydney Singapore

Books by Priscilla L. Vail, M.A.T.

Liberate Your Child's Learning Patterns
(Kaplan Publishing, 2002).

Homework Heroes, Grades K-2:
It's a Bird. It's a Plane. It's Done
(with Drew and Cynthia Johnson,
Kaplan Publishing, 2001).

Homework Heroes, Grades 3-5:
It's a Bird. It's a Plane. It's Done
(with Drew and Cynthia Johnson,
Kaplan Publishing, 2001).

Homework Heroes, Grades 6-8:
It's a Bird. It's a Plane. It's Done
(with Drew and Cynthia Johnson,
Kaplan Publishing, 2001).

Reading Comprehension:
Students' Needs and Teachers' Tools
(Modern Learning Press, 1999).

Language Assessment for Grades 3 & 4
(Modern Learning Press, 1998).

A Language Yardstick:
Understanding and Assessment
(Modern Learning Press, 1997).

"Words Fail Me":
*How Language Works and What Happens
When It Doesn't*
(Modern Learning Press, 1996).

Emotion:
The On/Off Switch for Learning
(Modern Learning Press, 1994).

Learning Styles:
*Food for Thought and 130 Practical Tips
for Teachers K-4*
(Modern Learning Press, 1992).

Common Ground:
*Whole Language and Phonics
Working Together*
(Modern Learning Press, 1991).

About Dyslexia:
Unraveling the Myth
(Modern Learning Press, 1990).

Smart Kids with School Problems:
Things to Know and Ways to Help
(NAL Plume Paperback, 1989).

Gifted, Precocious, or Just Plain Smart
(Modern Learning Press, 1987).

Clear & Lively Writing:
Language Games and Activities for Everyone
(Walker & Co., 1981).

The World of the Gifted Child
(Walker & Co., 1979).

Kaplan Publishing
Published by Simon & Schuster, Inc.
1230 Avenue of the Americas
New York, NY 10020

The chart of phonics-elements on page 40 is from *Recipe for Reading* by Nina Traub. Thanks to Educators Publishing Service for their kind permission to reprint it here.

Portions of the section, "At Promise/At Risk," in chapter four initially appeared in the *Newsletter of the New York Branch of The International Dyslexia Association*, 1998–99.

For bulk sales to schools, colleges, and universities, please contact: Order Department, Simon & Schuster, Inc., 100 Front Street, Riverside, NJ 08075. Phone: (800) 223-2336. Fax: (800) 943-9831.

For information regarding special discounts for other bulk purchases, please contact Simon & Schuster Special Sales at 1-800-456-6798 or business@simonandschuster.com

Kaplan ® is a registered trademark of Kaplan, Inc.

Cover Design by Cheung Tai
Book Design by Lili Schwartz
Editor: Beth Grupper

Manufactured in the United States of America
September 2002
10   9   8   7   6   5   4   3   2   1
Library of Congress Cataloging-in-Publication Data

ISBN: 0-7432-3052-3

To the Allen Stevenson School:
colleagues, students, parents,
with admiration, affection, and thanks
for my place among you.

■   ■   ■

ACKNOWLEDGMENTS

Particular thanks to:
my family, models and mentors;
the blessings of Bedford, spoken and unspoken;
the magic of Stonington, its readers and revelers;
the delicious distractions from A to Z that carbonate my life;
the teachers, students, and parents with whom I've developed
the strategies in this book, from whom I've learned,
and for whom I write.
—P.L.V.

■   ■   ■

CONTENTS

READING FOR MEANING–
THE MEANING OF READING

Do children need instruction in reading comprehension?
Definitely.
Are they receiving it?
Insufficiently.
Can it be taught?
Yes.
Can parents play an important role?
Yes.

For reading to be worth the time and effort involved, it must convey meaning, information, emotion, suspense, or similar delights. But increasing numbers of children—across geography, grades, and socio-economic levels—"bark at print" or dutifully rake their eyes across lines of words, absorbing little or nothing.

Many such children lack accurate skills for decoding (reading) big new words and are left to guess. Some approach muscular passages with scrawny vocabulary. Others plod concretely through inference, reading word for word, missing nuance, overlooking such indicators as *but, although,* or *on the other hand.* A large number misunderstand figures of speech, simile, metaphor, or analogy. And there are those who leave new concepts or facts lying on the page, undigested, because they haven't learned techniques for making new information memorable.

As a parent, your role in helping your child become an effective and enthusiastic reader begins with diligence at home. As you read with your child, be on the lookout for the following signs of reading discomfort:

- Your child doesn't understand what he reads.
- Your child doesn't know that he doesn't understand what he is reading.
- Your child doesn't think that it matters as long as he spends his homework hours holding onto a book.
- Your child doesn't choose reading—ever or rarely—over other forms of entertainment (television, video games, etc.).

Simultaneously, you should be aware of well-intentioned teachers who:

- don't understand the foundations of reading comprehension themselves, and therefore,
- don't know how to teach reading comprehension, and
- don't think teachers need to teach reading after second grade.

These patterns may be malevolent fallout from inadequate teacher training or from moth-eaten systems of instruction.

In learning to read, your child needed to see the connection between spoken language and printed words on the page. The next step is to bond the mechanics of reading skills with the meaning of written words, sentences, paragraphs, pages, or chapters. In other words, your child moves from learning to read to reading to learn.

Four Precepts

Four major precepts will focus our common purpose:

1. We (children, parents, and teachers) must be able to answer, "What is reading?" Reading is more than osmosis; it harnesses

multiple systems: eyes, ears, muscles, emotion, experience, psychological and intellectual availability, curiosity, and the stamina to keep on converting print into meaning.

2. Comprehension must embrace the entire curriculum—and extracurricular life, as well. It is much more than a splinter skill for language arts class.

3. We must infect children with what master teacher John Fennell calls "the contagion of nonpoisonous passions."

4. In this era of swiftly shifting visual stimulation, when electronic floodgates release deluges of information, we must continue to emphasize comprehension. Glimpsing is not the same as grasping.

Three Types of Reading

Many children—not to mention adults—aren't aware that there are different kinds of reading, each with its own rules, rigors, and taboos:

- factual/accuracy reading
- survey/text reading
- aesthetic/imaginative reading

Recognizing how we as adults shift among these three helps us see how they enfold or threaten younger readers. To me, beadwork, a smorgasbord, and ballroom dancing are images for these categories. Skillful writers may want to weave all three types together, but not all genres allow such combinations, and not all writers are skillful—or kind.

Factual/Accuracy Reading is like beadwork, slow and requiring accuracy. Readers use vigilance, patience, and logic to string the metaphoric red bead in the proper sequence on the thread. If you are an adult trying to register your car, the bureau of motor vehicles doesn't want to know that your machine is the same color as your eyes, or that the backseat is big enough to carry your mother-in-law in between the kids. The bureaucrat—or scanner—wants to know the make, year, color, and license number of your car, as well as your name, address, and zip code. Readers who omit answers or print information in the incorrect box will simply have to try again, while the car, unregistered, languishes in the garage.

Your child faces similar factual/accuracy tasks daily, as she follows directions on work sheets, solves math word problems, or takes tests.

Survey/Text Reading is like selecting food at a smorgasbord. The reader looks over the whole spread of offerings, choosing a bit here, a dollop there, or a metaphoric big piece of bread on which to lay the sardines, cheese, onion, tomato, or hearty slab of brisket with mustard—with or without horseradish. To make such choices, the reader must be familiar with the taste and texture of the individual dishes—remember that chocolate pudding doesn't go with pickles—and know which bring nourishment, which are garnish, and which unfamiliar possibilities might be worth a try.

To assemble a tasty, nourishing, perhaps even healthy mental meal of good ideas, the reader must fit compatible ingredients into an overall plan. If the topic is violent weather systems, an article on hemlines—no matter how interesting or well written—doesn't belong.

In order to be an effective survey/text reader, your child needs to learn ways to integrate incoming information, digest new ideas, and decide how and why to put some thoughts aside for later nibbles, treats, or main courses.

Whether we are third graders researching the explorers, or golden oldies or boomers delving into a survey of health care

plans, or people of any age tackling *A Beginner's Guide to the Trojan War*, readers investigating new information need:
- strategies to organize vocabulary
- connotations to make new material meaningful
- links to join the new to the familiar

Trying to connect unknowns with other unknowns doesn't work.

Aesthetic/Pleasure Reading is like a tango danced by writer and reader, who dip and sway together in rhythm to the words, the cadences, the themes. The dance may be slow, seductive, passionate, fast, flirtatious, teasing, humorous, energetic, or sultry. The dancers, embracing or mirroring across a distance, move as one. As the old saying goes, It takes two to tango.

Some readers enjoy lingering over phrases or descriptions; others surge through, arriving flushed and breathless at the end. Either way is correct. The writer invites the reader to dance. The reader sets the tempo, resonates to the images, and identifies with the characters. Such *choices* belong to the reader; the *words* belong to the writer. They must dance together, holding identical words, sharing common purpose.

The following quotes from literature and science substantiate—and summarize—the three types of reading:

About factual/accuracy reading. Over the front door to the Harvard Medical School is a quote from Louis Pasteur: "Chance favors the prepared mind."

About survey/text reading. E. M. Forster wrote, in *Howards End*, "Only connect!"

About the power of aesthetic/imaginative realms. Albert Einstein wrote, "My gift for fantasy has meant more to me than my capacity to acquire positive information."

A Six-Step Progression

Reading unfolds this way:
1. pre-reading
2. beginning reading
3. emergent reading
4. *con*tent reading
5. con*tent* reading
6. nimble reading

The pre-reader *gathers*: vocabulary; an understanding that print is speech mapped onto paper; that letters are symbols for sounds and that words are symbols for people, things, information, and feelings; that print confers permanence; and that writing and reading are a code.

The beginning reader *learns*: to recognize some words by sight, to use the code for both decoding (reading) and encoding (spelling), to enjoy one of the major secrets of the adult world.

The emergent reader *bonds with*: characters in stories, information on pages, questions, and narrative.

The *con*tent reader *absorbs*: stories of people, explanations of facts, directions for procedures, and information about how the world works. As deciphering the code becomes increasingly automatic, content becomes ever more accessible.

The con*tent* reader *harnesses*: rudimentary and sophisticated levels of phonics, word recognition, and vocabulary; general information; prowess in visual, auditory, and motor areas; emotional availability and optimism; comfort in using print for discovery.

The nimble reader *leaps*: into information, through concepts, alongside narrative, over and under conceptual challenges, and inside the mysteries and majesties of language.

Seven Elements of Comprehension

To travel the progression listed above, your child needs seven elements of comprehension:

1. definition
2. foundation
3. evaluation
4. instruction
5. participation
6. intuition
7. emancipation

Familiarity with these seven overlapping elements of reading comprehension will help you solidify your own knowledge before you start coaching your child. And because of their individual and collective importance, each of these seven elements earns a full chapter. Hence, the organization of this book.

All chapters contain the following common, internal organization:

At Promise/At Risk: An overview of the topic, why it matters, what happens in its absence.

Goals: What to aim for.

Tools: How to get there.

Landmines: What to watch out for, how to spot trouble.

VAIL: General principles of good practice. At the risk of seeming vainglorious, the acronym VAIL shows how to proceed:

> **V: Visualize.** For comprehension, readers need to make their own imagery.
>
> **A: Anticipate.** For comprehension, readers need to have a hunch of what's to come.
>
> **I: Interpret.** For comprehension, readers need to know what genre they are in.
>
> **L: Listen.** For comprehension, readers need to listen to the music of the writing.

Evidence: A sample.

Thus, you can read the book chapter by chapter, or you can follow a particular strand all the way through.

While specific suggestions for ages and grade levels are laced throughout the book, it is not designed to be a complete curriculum. While the book is designed to be informative, illustrative, and practical, it does not pretend to be all-inclusive.

Rather, the emphasis is on the spiral, cumulative aspects of comprehension.

By understanding the underpinnings of reading and by using the games and activities in this book, you will be well equipped to help solidify your child's reading comprehension skills.

Four Fundamentals

Four fundamentals surface throughout:

1. Emotion is the on/off switch for learning. Children who are frightened of reading approach print timidly, hesitantly, reluctantly—or angrily, resentfully, suspiciously. You need to help make reading safe, particularly if your child is dyslexic or has had a rough or unsuccessful beginning. Specific techniques are in my book, *Common Ground*.

2. The process of developing effective reading skills is like a carefully constructed spiral, always circling to higher levels, while also enfolding and incorporating earlier precepts.

3. Most children need direct instruction in both the structure and texture of reading all the way through. Communicate with your child's teacher to find out how he is receiving this instruction at school. You may be able to incorporate elements of the teacher's reading program into what you are doing at home, or the teacher might provide some insight into areas of strength and/or weakness for your child.

4. Comprehension is reading for meaning—the meaning of reading. In our electronic era, students must differentiate between having access to information and knowing how to use knowledge. Downloading is not the same as deliberating.

Writers often reveal their own comprehension problems. Recently, I received this note:

"I hear you're writing a book about reading comprehension. Please use all your *expert tease*."

CHAPTER 1

DEFINITION

At Promise/At Risk

The word *comprehension* comes from the Latin word *prehendere*, meaning to "seize, grab, or pick up." To some observers, reading seems like a passive activity because readers are either usually sitting, lolling, or curled up in bed. True reading, however, is highly active. A "passive seizer" is an oxymoron.

For comprehension to connect the writer and the reader, the reader must seize the same word the writer has written. Grabbing *for* instead of *from* will muddle up a gift—who's the *giver?* The reader must know the meaning of the single words in order to understand the whole text in which the words are embedded.

In *Through the Looking Glass*, Humpty Dumpty says to Alice, "When *I* use a word, it means just what I choose it to mean—neither more nor less." Humpty Dumpty thinks words have different motives and personalities: Although he believes you can push adjectives around, he maintains that verbs have tempers and are stubborn and proud. He vaunts, "*I* can use the whole lot of them. Impenetrability!" When Alice asks what *that* means, Humpty

Dumpty covers his tracks with a brusque "I mean by 'impenetrability' that we've had quite enough of that subject . . . "

Later on, Alice asks Humpty Dumpty to explain the meanings of such words as *brillig* and *slithy* from the poem "Jabberwocky." Exemplifying the old English adage, "often in error but never in doubt," he rattles off a series of intricately specific, deliciously preposterous definitions.

Such antics are fine in fiction, but actual readers need to *prehendere* the real stuff. Readers are interpreters, not inventors.

Goals

1. Demystify. When your child is taught phonics or word recognition, the definition of goals is clear, and whether he has reached them or not is obvious. Comprehension appears to be hazier, less specific, more subjective. Problems in interpretation are more filmy, shadowy, gauzy. Errors may persist, uncorrected or overlooked, particularly if your child's behavior is not disruptive or he does not call attention to himself. Unrecognized and unaided, this ersatz reader (your child) slides around in twilight zones of confusion and misdirection. By defining the elements of comprehension, we move away from smarmy, feel-good, warm-water wallowing to the crispness and strength comprehension requires and promises. Through definition, we demystify; through demystifying, we define.

2. Demonstrate. First and frighteningly, if I am going to demystify comprehension and demonstrate paths to mastery, I myself will have to write clearly. I will try.

Perhaps my courage to tackle such a daunting task as writing this book comes from a reader's response to an article I wrote:

"I love your stuff. You always hit the nose on the nail."

In turn, the ensuing strategies will help you demonstrate the how's and why's of comprehension to your child. Simultaneously, we must define our destination. As the old saying goes, If you don't know where you're going, any road will take you.

3. Define. To define the role of the reading coach—your role—is to launch a focused effort.

Before setting out, you must know:

- what you are trying to impart, and
- why your child needs this information.

With this clearly stated and understood by you and your child together, you can take the role of coach, delegating to your child the chance to put the ideas and strategies to work.

Tools

Helping Your Child Remember What She Reads

When you ask your child questions about a book or story she is reading, does she often say, "I don't remember"?

Sometimes, that's accurate, but frequently your child didn't *forget*: The information never stuck to begin with. Information sticks in memory when it is soaked in a three-part glue:

1. emotion,
2. experience, and
3. expression.

Let's see how that might pertain to a third-grade story about Native American culture. Your child might meet such new vocabulary as *tepee, wigwam, hogan, bluff, prairie, plain.* Sounding them out or recognizing them is a good beginning, but the words must also carry clear meaning. In cases of multiple meanings, the reader must make the appropriate choice. Is *bluff* a cliff or a poker strategy? Does *plain* mean flatland, unadorned, or homely?

When reading a story with your child, you should reassure her that some of these words are new and not everyone is supposed to know them. This establishes an emotional climate in which not knowing is fine. The next process is to show pictures and offer definitions, and have your child make her own labeled drawing of the new words. Making and labeling one's own drawing embeds the word in memory, and the drawing can be called upon for reference and reminder. You might even want to create a binder or scrapbook for your child's drawings so she can find them easily. Your child should then have an opportunity to display and explain the drawings to you in her own words.

Reading when the vocabulary is half-understood jeopardizes both comprehension and memory. Yet busy teachers with a lot of information to cover may not be aware of, or have time to focus on, this obstacle to comprehension.

Once the vocabulary is meaningful, your child can proceed to read information using the new words, and soak the new information in the three-part glue of emotion, experience, and expression. As your child reads more about Native American food, for example, you might discuss with her how the food we eat today is the same or different from the foods she is reading about, perhaps actually cooking something with corn. These conversations can also create a climate of emotional safety in the midst of excitement and exploration.

Next, your child needs chances to make drawings or dioramas of what she is learning. Finally, she needs to show and explain, telling about her products in her own words.

The joining of emotion, experience, and language enhances memory. Items lodged in memory are available for contemplation, thus comprehension. This applies equally to the intertwining categories of factual/accuracy reading, survey/text reading, and aesthetic/imaginative reading. Let's consider each type.

Tools for Factual/Accuracy Reading Comprehension

Many additional strategies follow throughout the book, but here's a general one for a successful, happy start.

Create a Daily Message bulletin board (or post the message on your refrigerator or other public family spot). Each day, write a message that informs your child about events of the day, particular instructions, and congratulations when appropriate. For example:

> *Today is Tuesday, so Dad will drop you off at the school bus and Mom will pick you up after school. Make sure you pack your permission slip for the school trip. You have soccer practice tonight, so please do your homework right after school. You did a great job on your spelling test this week!*

Give your child enough time to process the information thoroughly and talk about anything potentially confusing, settling such issues as which exit he'll be picked up at after school and what time soccer practice starts. And once your child becomes accustomed to looking for errors in grammar and spelling deliberately included in the message, you can warn him that the messages are going to include nonsense surprises as well. Factual/accuracy comprehension is, after all, simply a matter of focusing on detail. For example, one message might read:

> *Today is Tuesday, so Dad will drop you off at the school bus and Mom will pick you up after school. Make sure you pack your permission slip for the school trip. I put your blue slippers in your lunch bag. You have soccer practice tonight, so please do your homework right after school. You did a great job on your spelling test this week!*

Looking for a trick in the message enhances both vigilance and fun.

Tools for Survey/Text Reading Comprehension

To assimilate chunks of new information, your child needs to build internal scaffolds on which to hang incoming facts and ideas.

Using the title, chapter headings, and the glossary, she needs to predict some of the topics and outcomes in the books she reads. With such preparation, the actual reading becomes a binary game of "Yes, I thought of that," and "No, I didn't think of that."

When working on reading comprehension with your child, at the start of every paragraph, have her write on a piece of paper the key words in the topic sentence, and at the end of each paragraph, she should jot down a one-sentence summary. At the end of the story, your child should review the paragraphs in order, noting both the key words and the summaries. Or, for variety, recap the material first by reading the key words in sequence, then reading the summaries all the way through.

Tools for Aesthetic/Imaginative Reading Comprehension

Capturing Imagery. Today's children have few opportunities to create their own imagery; television and movies do it for them. And yet, internal pictures are what connect words and readers (or listeners) in that combination of intimacy and privacy known as comprehension.

You can offer this chance and challenge by first asking your child to close his eyes, then reading him a poem and asking him to see the words or phrases in his mind's eye. At the end, he should draw a picture—or jot or say a distillation—of his most captivating image.

Landmines

Understanding seven main areas of potential reading difficulty refines our definition of comprehension.

Mechanical: The child doesn't have the tools for decoding.

Visual: The child has trouble remembering and recognizing sight words (everyday words we recognize without stopping to sound them out, such as *the*). See appendix A for the Dolch Basic Sight Word List, which includes 220 high-frequency sight words.

Auditory: The child doesn't hear the sequence of sounds inside words correctly, and thus may have trouble blending sounds together or "sounding out."

Linguistic: The child may have a sparse vocabulary and not understand words even when decoding them correctly.

Hereditary: Learning patterns and styles are heavily influenced by genetics. A child with reading difficulties in her family is at risk for "more of the same."

Dyspedagogical: *Dys* means "difficulty with," *pedagogy* means "teaching." Some perfectly intact children have had minimal, mediocre, or insufficient reading instruction.

Developmental: Some schools that pride themselves on academic rigor boast that they use fifth- or sixth-grade materials for their third or fourth graders. If this is true at your child's school, he may appear to have problems, but the true problem is with a curriculum that is not age-appropriate.

Because the last three and the first three are equally integral to issues surrounding comprehension, they belong in any discussion of definition. Once you understand the differences among these potential difficulties, you can plan on-target help.

Which children have troubles in reading comprehension?

Eye Rakers: These are kids whose eyes rake along lines of print, but who don't generate imagery or soak new information in memory glue. At the end of ten minutes, they may say, "Okay, I've read it," because they were sitting obediently. But nothing penetrated.

Hiccuppers: These kids read without rhythm, moving forward four or five words, backing up, reading two or three again, then forging on, and jerking back. Sitting across from such a reader (so as to watch eye movements), we can see what look like visual hiccups.

Cool Dudes: These kids lug around thick books that are too hard for them to read, hoping to look "cool."

Pictureless Windows and Silent Musicians: These kids don't make or see the imagery in reading, nor do they hear the cadence of the words. Thus, they cannot flow with the rhythm.

Whole-to-Parters: Some learners need to understand the whole picture before they can understand, interpret, remember, or use what they read. They need to preview.

Humpty-Dumpties: These kids pretend to catch on to what they don't understand.

VAIL

Let's see how our acronym applies:

V: Visualize. Throughout this book, you will see the connections between comprehension and personal imagery and learn how to pass that along to your child.

A: Anticipating and previewing help your child build scaffolding for new information.

I: Interpreting opens the way to precision, connection, memory, and enjoyment.

L: Listen. Words make music. Music attaches to lyrics. Listen and learn.

Evidence

Sometimes, the fault lies with the writer, not the reader:

TEACHER STRIKES IDLE KIDS

CHAPTER 2

FOUNDATION

At Promise/At Risk

It's even in the Bible: build on rock, not sand. Yet many of today's children never learned the foundations of strong reading. Untaught, they try to build on quicksand. Accuracy and understanding collapse under curricular demands, and comprehension sinks in muddy suction and implosion. Busy teachers, with a lot of information to cover in class, may overlook reading difficulties or miss flaws in the foundation. Reading becomes an externally imposed burden, alternately meaningless and dangerous. Children slither along an unreliable surface or drown for want of a foothold.

Goals

Prevention is always easier than remediation. We need to build solid foundations for the 20 percent, 60 percent, and 20 percent.

Who?

The classic bell curve below—in segments of 20 percent, 60 percent, and 20 percent—represents the distribution of student-reader skills and offers powerful insights about reading instruction.

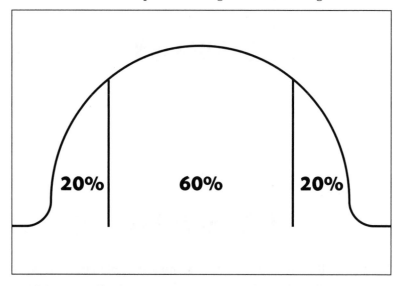

We can call the right-hand 20 percent of the bell curve the Space Bubble Kids. These are children who learn to decode and comprehend on their own. If they were left in a space bubble from birth until age seven, they would emerge knowing how to count, read, and spell. They would have figured it all out from the control panel. (If anyone is worried that I lock babies in space bubbles for statistical studies, this is a j-o-k-e.)

Research shows us, however, that even these seemingly autonomous readers need direct instruction in the basics, in order to maintain their own fast pace after mastering initial levels.

The 20 percent of students on the left-hand side of the bell curve are as easy to identify as the Space Bubble Kids. These young learners need extra teaching, additional practice, and multisensory methods and materials that combine seeing, hearing, and writing, as they struggle to crack the code of print.

This leaves 60 percent of children in the middle. We now know that of this 60 percent, roughly 70 percent will not and cannot intuit the rules of reading independently. Beginning with instruction in reading readiness and early mastery, they need to be taught the how's, the what's, and the why's of more complex levels. If they do not receive the teaching they need, they slip to the left, appearing to be part of the needier 20 percent. In fact, they are perfectly intact. These are the children who flounder when teachers don't recognize flaws in the foundation, and when inexperienced adults chant the mad-cow mantra that "things will take care of themselves."

This group needs our attention but has often been taken for granted by busy or unenlightened teachers.

Wherever your child falls in the distribution of student-reader skills, there are steps you can take to help him solidify his reading comprehension foundation.

Tools

Tools for Factual/Accuracy Reading Comprehension

You can:

1. Probe for automatic knowledge of sound/symbol correspondence, which means knowing the sounds of single letters and such letter combinations as *ai, eu, aw, ing, ild, ost, igh*. Specific suggestions follow in the next chapter, "Evaluation."

2. Review and practice the difference between long and short vowels.

3. Use listening and clapping, and offer frequent exercises in hearing and separating syllables. For example, "I am going to say a word. Repeat it softly to yourself, breaking it into chunks, which are called syllables. When I say 'Go,' hold up the number of fingers to match the number of syllables."

Start with easy words: *catnip, daytime, shoelace, finger, elbow, eyebrow.* Move to harder words: *hamburger, cellophane, computer, alphabet.* When your child can manage these, move to four- and five-syllable words: *aquarium, escalator, elevator, interpreter, arithmetic, division, multiplication, designation, destination, upholstery.*

Your child does not need to be familiar with all the words. In fact, it's good for practice—and for helping you uncover potential problem areas—to throw in some unknowns. Research shows that children who cannot break down words into their component sounds have difficulty blending sounds together in words they try to read or spell.

Slapjack. Adapting the old-fashioned game of Slapjack is an ideal way to strengthen rapid, accurate reading of individual words.

In this card game, one type of card is the stimulus: perhaps a jack, a two, or a ten.

In this adaptation, using colored index cards cut in half, write thirteen words, four times apiece, one word per card, making a total of fifty-two cards. The word list could include such high-frequency look-alikes as *for, from, if, of, when, where, who, how, what, why, with, which, whether.*

You'll be the dealer. Designate one word as "it." Display the cards one at a time, and your child must slap only the designated card when it appears. You can vary the speed and the number of players as proficiency dictates. In this game, as in all others, the goal is your child's success.

You can use this same format for the look-alikes *though, through, throughout, thought, thorough.* Write each one ten times for a fifty-card deck.

Also, use color coding to make a master chart of these words. (Your kid should practice with the master chart before playing the Slapjack game. Otherwise, the game may be too discouraging.) To make the master chart:

1. Choose one color for the letters in the word *though*. Write that word in a single color, color #1.

2. Write the word *through*, using color #1 for *t, h, o, u, g, h,* and a new color, color #2, for the letter (illustrated below with different backgrounds).

3. Write the word *throughout*, using color #1 for *t, h, o, u, g, h,* color #2 for *r*, and a new color, color #3, for *o, u, t*.

4. Write the word *thought*, using color #1 for *t, h, o, u, g, h,* and a new color, color #4 for the final *t*.

5. Write the word *thorough*. Write *t, h, o, u, g, h* in color #1, and *o, r* in a new color, color #5.

You can also use Slapjack for math-process words: *add, subtract, multiply, divide, total, difference, sum, product, remainder, left, overall, all together*. The stimulus for play would be "a word that means increase," "a word that means decrease," and so on. You can also adapt this format to process signs, writing each one ten times for a deck of fifty cards: +, –, x, ÷, =. Your child must call out the word that matches the sign, as well as slap only the stimulus. It is amazing how many math errors aren't math errors at all. They are caused by careless reading of process signs.

It would also be wise to make a color-coded chart of math words. Using three pieces of paper, write the words that indicate *increase* in green (the color of growth) on one piece of paper. On the next, write the words indicating *decrease* in red. On the third piece, write the terms indicating *ratio* or *equal* in blue. These helping hints should be used for as long as your child needs them.

Adapt any of the above to games of Concentration or Go Fish.

Tools for Survey/Text Reading Comprehension

Skim, shop, select, chunk, summarize, sort, file, retrieve, use, combine. Readers harness these ten verbs when tackling a newspaper, a textbook, a research project, a new concept, or a period in history. Let's take them individually. Then we'll see how to practice these skills with your child, using a single example to incorporate all ten.

Skim. In deciding which newspaper articles to read, which to skip, and which to save for later (How often does "later" really come?), we let our eyes roam over the possibilities rather like the way we use a mouse or trackball to zoom around a computer screen.

Shop. When we light on an appealing topic—an idea that reverberates or connects with something we've already learned, or an idea that catches our interest—we stop and shop. We read further in the article to see whether it fulfills its initial promise, whether it offers anything new, or whether it, perchance, contradicts what we thought.

To skim and shop profitably, we need to have a supply of general knowledge. Previous knowledge lets us choose, and it provides scaffolding on which to hang incoming information.

Select. Now, we are ready to refine our focus, selecting the information that will contribute to what we are trying to find out. We combine our reading and thinking into three hierarchical categories—major, minor, and mediocre—which author Madeleine L'Engle calls "majah, minah, and mediocah."

These three verbs, (*skim, shop, select*) tell us that readers need time to scroll up what they already think or know about a topic before trying to absorb new information. This is *metacognitive preparation*: thinking how we are going to be thinking about what we are going to think about once we start thinking about what we are going to be thinking about. New information sticks when it connects with what is already familiar.

Chunk. Readers moving around in single texts—or joining information from various sources—need to combine the information in chunks, so that bits and pieces stick together.

Summarize. Readers who amass combinations of information need to summarize as they go along. The process of distillation helps memory.

Sort. As readers skim, shop, select, chunk, and summarize, they need to sort the collected information, just as we divide the laundry. If we jam a sock, a dishtowel, a baseball shirt, dinner napkins, bath towels, and underpants into one load in the washing machine, we'll have a hard time getting dressed, setting the table, and playing on the field. Like Maytag mavens or Whirlpool wizards, readers need to sort information by categories.

File. Once information is in chunks, summarized and sorted, readers must file. Using such precision tools as categorization, human brains are highly efficient filing cabinets.

Retrieve. We can easily retrieve well-filed information. Back to laundry imagery, if we throw a neon pink T-shirt into the washing machine along with navy sweatpants, a white nightgown, car washing rags, and a bathroom rug, we will spend hours and muscles untwisting and untangling them after the spin dry.

Doubtless, the colors will have bled onto one another, turning everything gray. The same is true with thoughts and information. Crisp retrieval depends on appropriate filing.

Use. The purpose of acquiring information is to use it. Readers can use it best when it is in digestible chunks, easily separated and categorized, so that saliency is evident and meaning enhanced.

Combine. The ability to make novel combinations is a hallmark of intelligence, and a function unique to human beings, as far as we know. Creativity joins familiar elements in ways they have never been joined before.

You need to know this progression and help your child practice it. Let's try a sample topic, appropriate for third grade on up.

The topic: How did the invention of the automobile influence life?

You might start by asking your child what he already knows or can imagine about life before automobiles, writing correct or incorrect assumptions on a piece of paper and then discussing them. Together *skim* the topic, looking over drawings, books, articles, graphs, and/or photographs that you have collected. You and your child might discuss pre-automobile medicine, education, or opportunities to socialize.

After skimming the materials, have your child *shop* through the collection of ideas and tangible effects and then *select* (mentally or physically) the ones of greatest interest. Your child might be interested in how an automobile manufacturing plant operates. Or he might consider fashions of car design: large, small, sporty, with and without fins, colors. As your child peruses, reads, or interprets, he would *chunk* the information. For example, he might compare auto body shape in military vehicles, family cars, and community emergency equipment such as ambulances and fire engines.

In some form, your child should capture his ideas on paper.

Accumulation is valuable. In the margin or on index cards, have your child *summarize* what he is learning as the intake process unfolds. Your child may want to use words, or he may prefer to draw pictures. As the collection of ideas and information grows, he must *sort* the information into categories and *file* in his brain what he has chunked, summarized, and sorted. Finally, ask your child to make a brief written or oral report. As he prepares his report, he will *retrieve* his supply of stored information in order to *use* the information and so that he can *combine* his new ideas with his own imagination and talents to create something new.

Tools for Aesthetic/Imaginative Reading Comprehension

For your child to be ready for comprehension in the imaginary realm, she first needs to remember that such a realm exists. Little children are accustomed to fanciful stories of talking animals, flying pigs, waltzing giraffes, ferocious (but safely imprisoned on the page) dragons and villains.

But sometimes, particularly in highly demanding schools, when children reach third grade and beyond, fantasy is replaced by reading assignments that emphasize following directions and explanations, and absorbing text and information. The best prompts to powerful comprehension in the imaginative realm are practice, permission, and familiarity. Fantasy is needed equally in upper grades and lower grades.

When your child starts out to read a story, she should flip around through the book, looking at illustrations, sampling vocabulary, testing the rhythm of sentences and the lengths of paragraphs. We adults must remember that this kind of reading is like a dance of author and reader together, and partnership should be a choice.

You should remember, and your child should know, the "three R's": *read, ruminate, respond.*

Read. This speaks for itself, but remember that reading flows more smoothly with anticipation and preparation.

Ruminate. Your child must be given time to imagine, to dream the story, to connect it with other stories, to join the hero or heroine with others from other stories.

Respond. Your child needs to make *active* responses: to invent alternative endings, to make a diorama, to pantomime, to paraphrase, to satirize. Your child needs an audience (you) and a response to her responses. While these take time, they infuse joy into a reading life.

Landmines

Slippery spoken language is a tip-off to confused comprehension. A teenager said, "No, I didn't go to the party. I lost my nerve. Besides, I hate those kinds of big parties. I just get lost in the shovel."

If you get lost in the shovel, it's hard to take the ball by the horns!

VAIL

V: Visualize. While reading about the princess and the dragon, or the first black cars, or while clapping the syllables in the word *computer,* give your child time to develop the habit of seeing his own imagery in his mind's eye.

A: Anticipate. Prediction sets the stage for comprehension. Familiarity with different genres (more to come on this in a later chapter) will help your child choose the correct mind-set for what's to come.

I: Interpret. Comprehension depends on melding your child's interpretation of text with the author's intent in writing.

L: Listen. Many readers improve their comprehension and memory by reading aloud. While this is no longer fashionable, if it works, use it.

Evidence

The student who read *excite* when the writer wrote *execute* got an unexpected jolt!

CHAPTER 3

EVALUATION

At Promise/At Risk

In our family, every year we give ourselves a treat/upgrade for our cherished seaside summerhouse. This particular year, it was to be *my* bathroom! All winter I fantasized about elbowroom, suds, thick towels, luxuries and toiletries, and deep hedonistic pleasures.

Oops.

Then came a rainstorm, followed by a phone call from the winter tenants to report a leak in the living room. I arranged to meet John DeCiantis, our house doctor and skillful contractor, on the site. He brought his favorite diagnostic instrument, a Swiss Army knife with its blades of all different shapes and sizes, including a marlin spike. But all he needed this time was his thumb.

We went upstairs and out onto the deck, which is located over the living room. It sits up off the roof by about twelve inches. John poked around the door leading to the deck, wove his number-two Eagle pencil through his thick salt-and-pepper hair, leaned over and thumped on the junctures of roof and sides of the house, shook his honest head, and looked sorrowful.

"Here's the story," he said. "Everything *looks* fine—you know—to your eyes. But the flashing is pulling away from the house, and so you've got rot under the clapboards. The roof is fifty-fifty shot. It's thirty-five years old. What we've got to do is dismantle the deck planking, jack up the frame, send the roofers underneath it to remove and replace this whole section of roof, remove the clapboards, strip and remove the flashing. While we're at it, we ought to hang some new gutters. After all that, we can finally put on a new fascia board and call in the painter. It may look pretty now, but it's full of rot. Rot creeps."

"And this will cost—?" I asked.

"I guess you know from the way you ask," he said, fixing me with his compassionate brown eyes. "It'll be about the same as that pretty bathroom you were planning. But you know as well as I do that deferred maintenance costs more in the long run. Face it, Mrs. Vail. Rot creeps."

The same is true in reading. Rot creeps.

Before we put metaphoric coats of new white paint on students' reading comprehension skills, we have to probe around with our academic Swiss Army knife. Curricular rainstorms may produce leaks. We may find moisture inside the flashing, we may have to replace some spongy timbers, we may have to cut and prime whole new fascia boards before we try to make the surface look pretty. Rot creeps.

Children whose reading instruction has been haphazard—who may have bounced around in whole-language classrooms with ad hoc phonics, who have been left to their own devices to figure out what reading comprehension is all about, or who have had teachers who are affectionate and attractive but untrained in the rudiments of reading instruction themselves—may manage in the early years. But starting in third grade and continuing throughout their education, they will flounder in the abstract aspects of reading.

You can help monitor your child's reading comprehension skills in order to determine if they are solid or if your child needs help.

Goals

Ideally, each year from first grade on up, you should develop a profile for your child, noting:

- emotional reaction to, and availability for, reading;
- knowledge and use of phonics;
- recognition of sight words;
- relative strengths in silent and oral reading;
- understanding and recall of passages, and connections to previous knowledge.

Can this miracle happen without devouring your schedule, driving you crazy, and breaking the budget? YES!

Tools

Use the following four tools to create your child's profile. (Note: the profile doesn't need to be completed in one sitting; you might prefer to do one part at a time.)

1. Transfer the list of phonic elements (found at the end of this chapter, on page 40) to a stack of cards, one element per card. Make a score sheet with the list of phonic elements on it. Go through the cards with your child, noting on the score sheet which sounds your child knows and which are not yet automatic.

2. Follow the same procedure for high-frequency sight words using the Dolch Basic Sight Word List in appendix A.

3. Ask your child's teacher whether there are any language-

screening devices in the classroom. If there are, ask for your child's results. (If there aren't, I developed my own, *Language Assessment for Grades 3 & 4,* which will provide you with everything you need. For younger children, see my book *A Language Yardstick.* Both are listed on the card page following the title page. You can find their publishers listed in appendix B.)

If your child touches bedrock in the above skills, he will be able to approach higher levels of reading with not only availability, but also enthusiasm.

4. Probe reading proficiency and comprehension in the following way: Find two short passages in a grade-normed elementary-school reader, a reading test, or other reliable source. Your child's teacher or a librarian can help you. Photocopy them and put one on a card marked "Oral," and the other on a card marked "Silent." Then devise ten questions for each, two apiece in the following five categories:

    1. fact retrieval

    2. sequence

    3. vocabulary

    4. main idea

    5. inference

For example, if the passage is about a boy going for a walk in the woods with his dog, the questions might be:

(Fact)

What was the name of the dog?

(Fact)

How old was the boy?

(Sequence)

What was the first thing the dog tried to chase in the woods?

(Sequence)

What did the boy do after the dog retrieved the stick?

(Vocabulary)

What does the word *scamper* mean?

(Vocabulary)

When the story talks about *brush,* does it mean something that goes with a comb?

(Main Idea)

Why do you think the title "A Surprise in the Woods" is a good one for this story?

(Main Idea)

How would the story have been different if the boy had taken a cat or a friend for the walk in the woods?

(Inference)

Does the boy have brothers and sisters, or is he an only child?

(Inference)

What part of the story makes you think that?

If the story doesn't have juicy vocabulary, add some more complex words. If the story is sparse on detail, insert some. Play with the text so that it offers interesting questions.

When the reading cards are ready and the questions composed, you'll need to make a score sheet similar to the one on pages 36 and 37. While this chart is rather elaborate, it is necessary in order to accurately screen your child.

If you discover that your child is stronger in oral reading and comprehension, share the news. You might say, "Here's a tip. When you come to something you really want to remember, read it aloud, even if you just whisper it to yourself. Sometimes, the combination of seeing with your own eyes and hearing your own voice with your own ears makes information stick."

Conversely, if your child is stronger in silent reading and comprehension, you might say, "Here's a tip. When you come to something you really want to remember, read it silently. Sometimes, the act of putting what you see into spoken words distracts from the meaning and makes it harder to remember."

READING COMPREHENSION SCORE SHEET

SILENT READING	high	average	low
Apparent comfort			
Speed			
Rhythm			

ORAL READING	high	average	low
Ease			
Speed			
Rhythm, inflection, expression			
Accuracy in word recognition or decoding,			
Use of punctuation for phrasing and meaning			

COMPREHENSION QUESTIONS IN SILENT READING

Mark a plus if your child answers the questions below correctly and a minus if your child answers the questions incorrectly.

___ Fact retrieval ___ Fact retrieval ___ Sequence ___ Sequence

___ Vocabulary ___ Vocabulary ___ Main idea ___ Main idea

___ Inference ___ Inference

COMPREHENSION QUESTIONS IN ORAL READING

Mark a plus if your child answers the questions below correctly and a minus if your child answers the questions incorrectly.

___ Fact retrieval   ___ Fact retrieval   ___ Sequence   ___ Sequence

___ Vocabulary   ___ Vocabulary   ___ Main idea   ___ Main idea

___ Inference   ___ Inference

Place a checkmark next to one of the following:

___ Comprehension stronger in Silent   ___ Comprehension stronger in Oral

Ask your child the following question and put a checkmark next to your child's response below:

Do either of these stories remind you of any other stories you have read or heard, or of something that may have happened to you?

___ Yes   ___ No

Child's overall comprehension is:

___ High   ___ Average   ___ Low

Child's attitude toward reading:

___ Child appears confident about reading
___ Child appears apprehensive about reading

Landmines

Missing Logic Alarms. Notice the absence or presence of a Logic Alarm System in your child. For example, beware of "it." When your child misreads a word or phrase, turning it senseless, you might say, "Does that make sense?" If your child replies, "No, but that's what *it* says," she is saying that she doesn't expect print or reading to be logical. Readers who are accustomed to sense and comprehension have a Logic Alarm System, which sounds gongs and whistles when meaning escapes. Such a reader may make an error but will then back up and try again, feeling uncomfortable until sense reenters the picture.

Shift Skippers. As we saw in the introduction, readers who skip over such sense shifters as *but, although, on the other hand* are headed for misinterpretation.

Twisty Blinkers. If your child twists and fidgets, he is telling you he is uncomfortable. Hair twisting, eye blinking, rocking, or making involuntary noises are noteworthy behaviors. In addition, readers in motion frequently skip lines, lose their places on the page, or may even turn two pages at a time and not notice the discontinuity.

Time Losers. Readers who haven't developed a gut-deep concept of time—who do not use past, present, and future verb tenses in their spontaneous speech—generally skip over temporal word endings (*ed, ing*) in reading, with disastrous results in comprehension. Description, comparison, and such devices as flashback all use (and depend on) the concept of time. Sequence, the skeletal structure of plot, vanishes in the absence of time.

Punctuation Passers. Punctuation divides text into meaningful units. Readers who skip punctuation don't know whether they are gourmets or cannibals:

"When are we going to eat Mother?"

VAIL

V: Visualize. In all genres you must encourage your child to "make a mental movie" of what is happening in the story or what the directions indicate. Giving your child time to turn his internal pictures into drawings or words protects these valuable visions from evanescence. When imagery sticks, comprehension solidifies.

A: Anticipate. By reading the title and developing a hunch of what's to come, your child will establish a conceptual grid and hooks for new information. If your child has a reading assignment for homework, encourage him to read the comprehension questions before he reads the text. The questions will tell your child what the writer thinks is important.

I: Interpret. Teach your kid to link each sentence with the one that came before and to link each paragraph with its predecessor.

L: Listen. Teach your child to listen for the sense or non-sense of what he reads.

Evidence

Without evaluation, how can we know whether a reader can have "a *peek* experience"?

Phonics Sequence Chart[1]

c (hard as in *cat*)	Introducing Consonant	au (*August*)
o (*olive*)	Blends	a (*ball*)
a (*apple*)	Endings: ing, ang, ong,	oi (*oil*)
d	ung, ink, ank, onk, unk	oy (*boy*)
g (hard as in *go*)	Magic e (a–e, e–e, i–e,	tch (*catch*)
m	o–e, u–e)	*ing* as an Ending
l	ph (*phone*)	Suffix: ed
h	ea (*eat*)	ew (*grew*)
t	oa (*soap*)	eigh (*eight*)
i (*Indian*)	ai (*mail*)	ie (*chief*)
j	ee (*tree*)	eu (*Europe*)
k	ay (*play*)	ei (*ceiling*)
p	oe (*toe*)	tion (*action*)
ch (*chin*)	er (*her*)	ue (*rescue*)
u (*up*)	ir (*bird*)	sion (*division*)
b	ur (*burn*)	ow (*snow*)
r	ow (*clown*)	ch (*school*)
f	ou (*ouch*)	ea (*head*)
n	igh (*light*)	oo (*good*)
e (*egg*)	Endings: ble, fie, tia,	ew (*few*)
s (*sit*)	dle, gle, kle, ple, zie,	ei (*vein*)
sh	ild, old, ind, ost, olt	ue (*true*)
th (hard as in *that*)	ar (*star*)	ou (*group*)
w	or (*horn*)	sion (*mansion*)
wh	oo (*zoo*)	ea (*great*)
y (*yes*)	Endings: ly, vy, by, dy,	ch (*machine*)
v	ty, fy, ny, py, sy	s (*is*)
x	ck (*black*)	
z	ge, dge	
th (soft as in *thin*)	y as a Vowel	
qu (*queen*)	aw (*straw*)	

[1]This master list is from *Recipe for Reading* and is reproduced here with the kind permission of Educators Publishing Service.

CHAPTER 4

INSTRUCTION

At Promise/At Risk

Aargh! *#!+@#$! I heard it in the elevator at a teacher's conference. I promise. It's true. I couldn't make it up. An attractive, glossy-haired, bright-eyed teacher—the kind any kid would take a shine to—said, "*Teach* reading? I don't *teach* reading. By fourth grade, kids already know how to read. And for the ones who haven't got it all together yet, I just let them choose popular fiction books so they can look cool on the school bus, and I soak them in literature and response journals. I think they all catch up. Or I guess they do. You want to have lunch?"

This infectious attitude is responsible for an osteoporosis in the skeletal structure of kids' reading skills, a shrinkage of reasoning, a malnourishment of student intellect, an atrophy in teaching skills, and a paralysis in the teaching of reading and the reading of teaching.

While the initial phases of reading instruction belong appropriately in the early grades, needs don't stop just because students have learned to decode or encode vowel teams (such as *au, ie, ou*), because they can recognize 220 high-frequency words, or because they have been bathed in the rhythms of language by hearing stories read out loud. Remembering the 20 percent, 60 percent, 20 percent bell curve (see page 20), we see that most children need continuing, carefully sequenced, direct instruction in the increasingly complex skills, mysteries, and delights of reading as they progress through elementary school, high school, and even beyond.

Do you know the philosophy of your child's teacher or your school district toward continuing reading instruction beyond the initial stages? If you are coaching your child at home, here's what your child needs to learn and what you can do to help.

Goals

Here are five goals:

1. As we saw in chapter 3, your child needs reliable foundations in the mechanical mastery of the early levels: decoding, encoding, word recognition, syllabication (forming or dividing words into syllables).

2. Probe your child's language development levels to be sure prerequisites are in place, and consult her teachers for their observations about her development. Many math and science students who do well with numbers are flummoxed by word problems because they're not really sure of the meanings of *area, circumference, radius,* while others regularly scan the sky but neither use nor understand the words *nimbus, cumulus, cirrostratus, thunderhead,* or *vortex.*

3. Help your child preview what she is about to read (demonstrating how a good title gives a hint), predicting whether a passage is likely to be fact, science fiction, fairy tale, biography, or humor.

4. You should reinforce at home:

- how to use inference to understand what is implied, as well as what is stated;
- methods for remembering factual information;
- strategies for developing a mental time line to keep events in sequence, while detecting flashback or fast-forward;
- suggestions on how to identify and use the main idea.

It's not only the slower children who need direct instruction in these elements. Often, the brightest kids see interesting implications in seemingly mundane statements and enjoy meandering side-paths, not always sticking to the author's intended goals and purposes. For example, I was working with an eighth-grade boy who had trouble identifying the main idea in reading tests and exercises. I asked him if he knew why this was hard for him.

"Yeah," he said. "I know, but I don't want to say."

"Why?" I asked.

"Because you'd probably think it was dumb," he answered.

"Try me," I said.

"Okay. You see, I think ideas are kind of like people. They all have interesting things about them, not just the obvious ones. And I don't want to hurt any idea's feelings by saying it isn't a main one."

5. As your child reaches high school, college, and even that four-letter institution called *l-i-f-e*, he will still need to organize and remember what he reads, and retrieve what he is learning through reading. Only then can your child bring rich and varied contributions to the convergence zones of executive function (having an idea and working it through), working memory, and the miracle of human cognitive function.

Tools

Tools for Factual/Accuracy Reading Comprehension

Decoding and encoding are flip sides of the same coin. When we understand the patterns of spelling, our reading becomes more accurate, and vice versa. Help your child understand the following patterns. Let's play some games:

What's My Pattern? (seven structural generalizations; remember the old saying, Exceptions prove the rule.)

1. Ask your child, "When do we use: *al* or *le*? Think about nouns and adjectives." Then say, "Can you spot my rule in *a musical bicycle*? If you think you have figured out the rule, test it. Have you deduced *the principal principle*?"

(An administrator in charge of running a school is the major, most important teacher and therefore is the *principal* teacher. Usually, a good principal stands on *principle*.)

With your child, try to think of two additional examples.

2. Ask your child, "When do we use: *us* or *ous*? Think about nouns and adjectives again. Can you spot the pattern in *an enormous chorus*?" Try to think of two additional examples with your child.

3. Ask your child, "When do we use: *ar, or,* or *er*? Think about adjectives, think about who is the *doer*." (That was a hint.) "Can you spot the pattern in *popular doctors, actors, and painters*?" Isn't this spectacular? Try to find additional examples with your child.

4. Ask your child, "When do we use: *ge* or *dge*? Think about long and short vowels. Then try to spot the pattern in *a huge piece of fudge*. Does the rule work in *in a rage, the animal ran over the bridge and into the cage*?" Shall I badger you to find three more examples?

5. Ask your child, "When do we use: *ch* or *tch*? Think about the position of the sound in the word. Can you spot the pattern in *chop that batch*?" Here is a sentence containing a bunch of exceptions: *The rich have much with which to buy such sandwiches.*

6. Ask your child, "When do we use: *ck* or *k*? Think about the position of the sound in the word again. What happens if the word ends in silent *e*? Can you spot the pattern in *kick* or *the kangaroo can duck the muck and lick the stick*? How about *cake*?" With your child, try to find three more examples.

7. Ask your child, "When do we use: *ary* or *ery*?" This is really easy. Only one noun ends in *ery: stationery*!

Catch That Syllable. Each of the preceding chapters suggested ways to play with syllables. Building on these previous ideas and moving to a more complicated level, say a multisyllablic word, ask your child to count the syllables and then hold up a corresponding number of fingers. Then, ask your child to *repeat* the third syllable or the first or final one. As his accuracy improves, ask him to *write* the second or fourth syllable. Examples might include: *alligator*, four syllables, say the third: *ga*. (Note that the vowel is long, therefore, this is an open syllable.) Or try *peninsula*, four syllables, write the second: *in*.

For reasons no one seems to pinpoint, when children misread polysyllabic words, their errors are generally in the third syllable. Thus, it is wise to play with lots of four-, five-, or six-syllable words, or trot out the old standby: *supercalafragilisticexpealidocious*. There is plenty of room to play in that one!

For help finding multisyllablic words, use a standard dictionary; it will also show syllable breaks for every word.

Make It Up. Make up a list of nonsense words or syllables, using a box of magnetic or cardboard letters (or write them on a piece of paper), and ask your child to read them. If your child can decipher nonsense correctly, she is equipped to decode any new word! When your child is proficient at this level, make and pronounce a nonsense word. Your child must listen and spell the word, and then check the letters to see if she is correct. Repeat this exercise several times.

Thumb Reading. Teach your child to use his thumbs in decoding big, unfamiliar, or confusing words. Here's how. When your child meets a big new word, he should scan for familiar chunks such as *ing* or *ed* at the end, or *non* at the beginning. If there is a familiar chunk at the beginning, have him cover it with his left thumb, cover a familiar chunk at the end with his right thumb, and read what's left in the middle.

For example, if the word is *nonsmoking*, your child would cover *non* with his left thumb, *ing* with his right thumb, and read *smok* in the middle. (He can mentally add the silent *e*, making it *smoke*, because he knows the *e* would have been dropped before adding *ing*.)

Have your child try Thumb Reading these words: *indigestible*, *unmerited*, *ultralovable*, *hyperexplanatory*, or *superknowable*. Sure it's okay to invent. Word play is legal.

Get to the Root of the Matter. On a piece of paper, draw a tree: trunk and canopy. On the canopy, in random order, write different affixes in traffic light colors: green for prefixes (suggesting *go*), red for suffixes (suggesting *stop*). At the base of the trunk, put a stack of index cards, on each of which is written a root or base word. Have your child pick a root card, scan the supply of affixes, and add as many as possible to the root, writing each new word down on the index card, and earning one point for each affix.

For example, *super-know-able* would earn two points. *Un-re-pent-ing-ly* would earn four. Playing this game sharpens your child's understanding of word derivation, enhancing comprehension as well as expanding vocabulary.

Here are some roots and affixes to get you started. Roots: *geo, graph, thermo, astro.* Prefixes: *mis, re, un, pre.* Suffixes: *ment, able, ish, ly.* You will find more practice with roots and affixes in upcoming chapters.

Pig Latin. In addition to being fun, this eternally popular word play offers practice in knowing where sounds sit in words, a mainstay of accurate reading. In playing, the speaker moves the initial sound of a word to the end of the word, and adds *ay*. For example, the word *lake* becomes *ake-lay,* the word *mountain* becomes *ountain-may, computer* morphs into *omputer-cay,* and slang such as *in your dreams* becomes *in-ay our-yay eams-dray. Atch-cay? An-cay ou-yay ead-ray ese-thay: izza-pay, usic-may ox-bay, ilt-quay, ippopotamus-hay? Ongratulations-cay!*

Box It. Some children, bright though they may be, have trouble reading and following directions and instructions. They look at the black box at the top of a workbook page, ignore it, jump to the middle of the page, panic, and say, "I don't get it!" Or they whirl through a math problem, hoping the numbers will be enough. Here's a way to help:

Box It

Step One: DO NOT READ THE WORDS IN THE DIRECTIONS. Instead, skim along the line of print until reaching a period. Put a red line under the period, and in the upper right hand corner of the page, put a tally mark. Keep skimming the lines of print, marking each period with a red line, and adding a corresponding tally mark at the top of the page.

Step Two: Count the number of red marks under the periods, being sure they match the number of tally marks. This tells the number of segments in the set.

Step Three: Read the first sentence. STOP at the red mark. It is like a red traffic light. Visualize what you are supposed to do. When you are sure you have understood the meaning of the sentence, and have seen in your mind's eye how you are to proceed, cross off one tally mark. Read to the next red light. STOP. Be sure you understand all the words and what they mean individually, as well as collectively. Visualize what you are meant to do. When you are sure, check off the next tally mark. Continue in this way until all the tally marks are crossed off.

Step Four: Then—and only then—read the whole set of directions. Proceed. Succeed.

This strategy takes longer to explain than it takes to do. Children love it, and it focuses attention. Here's how. Give your child a red pen, telling her it is a special piece of equipment, only to be used for Box It, and she should reach for the red pen whenever she meets a set of directions or instructions. (This attention catcher emphasizes the importance of the exercise.)

Follow similar steps for reading and solving word problems in math. Have your child color code the process signs, as suggested in an earlier chapter, marking those which indicate expansion in green, and using red for contraction. Many math errors come from skipping or misinterpreting process signs.

In your child's notebook or binder, have her write the words in color for math problems: green for increase, red for decrease, blue for ratio. Brainstorm with your child. Elicit from her the words and phrases she meets frequently. Decide with your child which category and color these particular words fit. Allocate. Have her write them in her notebook. You will be surprised at how often you will hear your child say, "Oh, yes. That's a green word," and how frequently she checks the chart to be sure she is moving in the right direction.

Tools for Survey/Text Reading Comprehension

Approximately half the school population is made up of children who develop concepts by accumulating and assembling incremental bits of information; they are sequential, part-to-whole learners. The other half need to know the whole idea first and then enjoy breaking it down into components and reassembling it; these students are simultaneous, whole-to-part learners.

Students in the first group are comfortable reading traditionally arranged texts. The second half need to know what's coming and what facts and opinions they are going to need and use. Only then do they capture what are otherwise flyaway scraps of information. Yet roughly 75 percent of curriculum materials used in schools are written by sequential, part-to-whole thinkers for other sequential, part-to-whole thinkers. This leaves whole-to-part-to-whole readers and thinkers out of sync with their schoolwork.

If your child is a whole-to-part-to-whole thinker, here are some strategies you can share to help him turn his classroom materials inside-out.

Out of Order!

Have your child follow these seven steps before tackling a reading assignment:

Step One: Heading into a chapter of text or a new unit, have your child read the title, anticipate the subject matter, and then go straight to the conclusion.

Step Two: After reading the title and the conclusion, your child needs to hypothesize how the end will connect with the beginning.

Step Three: Your child should read any questions at the end. They show what the writer wants the reader to remember.

Step Four: Your child should study the glossary to become familiar with the terminology, names, and places.

Step Five: Starting at the beginning, your child should read the italicized headings all the way through.

Step Six: Your child should read the introductory paragraph(s) and reread the conclusion.

Step Seven: Your child should then read the whole text and answer the questions, locating the words or passages that provide the answers.

The Sum of the Parts. In real estate, there are three important considerations: location, location, and location. In reading comprehension (particularly to integrate large amounts of information), there are three requirements: summarize, summarize, and summarize.

Wading into a large topic, your child should keep a stack of index cards handy, with one card right beside the text. At the end of each paragraph, have him jot a word or phrase summing up the main point.

At the end of a section, your child should clip the index cards together, and on a cover card, write a four- or five-sentence summary of salient features. At the end of the whole chapter, have him put all the cards together and make one overall card summarizing the combined summaries.

Webbing. Standard teaching methods such as classical out-lining and note taking may or may not be comfortable or suc-cessful for everyone. Teach your child to make information webs (also called "mind maps"). Start with a blank, unlined piece of notebook paper. In the center, ask your child to draw a circle and write the overall topic inside the circle. Then have your child draw spokes extending from the center circle and new circles or spokes extending from the first spokes. These sec-ondary spokes and circles are for supporting information. Each secondary set of spokes or circles should sprout new spokes and circles. (See sample web on the next page). The point is to help your child use diagrams to tame and organize information in hierarchical categories.

The Six *wh* Words. Your child needs to be intimately aware of the six *wh* words. They are the spine connecting the limbs of comprehension: *who, what, when, where, why,* and *how.* Your child should develop the habit of asking and answering the six *wh* questions at the end of each chapter or segment.

Compost Heap. Remember the boy in the opening section of this chapter who didn't want to hurt the feelings of an idea by saying it wasn't the main one? In particular stages of develop-ment, generally into fifth grade and sometimes beyond, chil-dren are still gathering information as rapidly as possible. They are not ready to sort it out and throw it away. They are gleaners, not winnowers.

Reassure your child that there are safe places to store ideas, and that he can start and maintain an intellectual compost heap onto which he can toss provocative ideas, juicy vocabulary, philosophical questions, or anything else that catches his fancy. Some thoughts

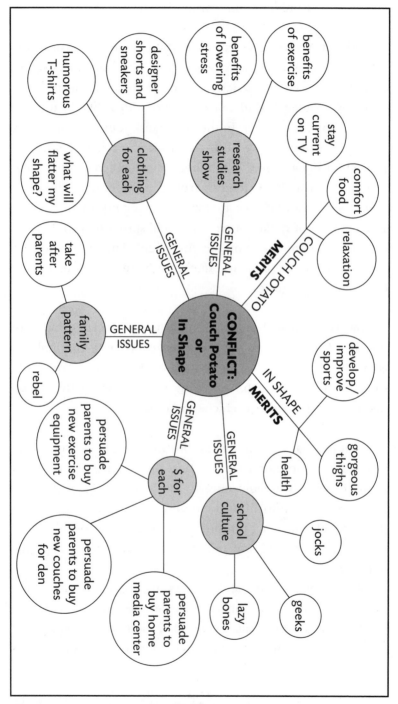

will be useful next week; others may lie there for six weeks, six months, or six years. The point is that they are in safekeeping, waiting to make their contribution when the time is right. Many children are greatly relieved to have a manila folder for this purpose. When anxiety over losing a good thought is reduced, your child (or this author!) doesn't have to keep trying to jam a favorite into a framework that doesn't fit.

Tools for Aesthetic/Imaginative Reading Comprehension

The three R's mentioned earlier explain what the reader in this genre needs to do: *read, ruminate,* and *respond.*

Read. It is important to offer your child a choice of reading material. If your child is in the mood for a mystery/adventure story, he will chafe at the imagery unfolding slowly in poetry. If your child is eager for the next installment in his favorite science fiction series, he will feel cheated by a collection of fairy tales. Your child needs exposure to many different genres, first by hearing them read aloud. He deserves to be in on the secret that there are many choices and flavors in reading.

And all school-age children deserve their own library cards!

Freedom to stalk the stacks is intoxicating. The great writer Eudora Welty tells about her own mother taking her at age six to the local library and introducing her to the librarian, saying, "This is my daughter, Eudora. She has my permission to read any book in this library *except* the Bobsey Twins."

Ruminate. Through rumination, your child will draw words, images, and ideas into that personal matrix some call *soul.* To ruminate and to translate take time. Hurried mulling is a contradiction in terms. You must carve out time in your child's schedule for this vital aspect of pleasure reading, even if it means accumulating fewer titles.

Respond. It is through making a product that your child will complete the circle of read, ruminate, respond.

Embodying all three R's, here is a trio of suggestions for increasing levels of competence:

Level one: Have your child read and illustrate, read and pantomime, or read and write a continuation of the story.

Level two: Have your child read and then make a storyboard, read and create a board game, or read and construct dioramas or stage sets.

Level three: Have your child read and record (variations on the standard book report), read and write a similar yarn (which requires deep understanding of the convention and construction of the original), or read and make a game of Essence about the book. Essence asks questions: If she were a musical instrument, what kind of instrument would she be? If he were a game, what game would he be? If she were food, what food would she be? The point is to capture the essence of the person, translating that essence into a new domain. Sometimes, people disagree. "No, Erica would never be a guitar! She's definitely the drums." Or, "Thomas could only be a folk song." Or, "To me, Jesse is a three-course feast, but on the other hand, he might be a picnic."

In true play, there are no right or wrong flights of fancy.

Landmines

"What?" is a tip-off that reading didn't stick. Maybe the reading was too hard. Maybe your child read the words inaccurately. Maybe she didn't have the overall idea. Maybe she couldn't immerse herself. As in:

INSTRUCTION

Your child: "What do you mean *except* the birthday present? I thought it said *expect!*"

Your child: "*Battle, ballet, ballot*—what's the difference? They're all the same to me. I read for a whole half hour."

You: "Tell me about the dragon in the cave."

Your child: "What dragon?"

VAIL

V: Visualize. Stories become vivid through vision. You must reward the creation of imagery by offering opportunities for your child to share what he has *seen* in the words he read.

A: Anticipate. Predictive structure (whether part-to-whole or whole-to-part) provides a metaphoric strip of Velcro to which new ideas and information stick.

I: Interpret. The difference between a joke and a letter to the editor is framed by vocabulary and sentence structure. When your child interprets correctly, she is rewarded with both laughter and learning.

L: Listen. A joke and a letter to the editor not only look different, they *sound* different. When your child listens with his ears to what he is seeing with his eyes, he will intensify the glories of meeting words on a page.

Evidence

Sign at a fund-raising bake sale:
KEEP OUR SOCCER TEAM UNDERFEETED

CHAPTER 5

PARTICIPATION

At Promise/At Risk

Print offers words, sentences, paragraphs, sections, chapters, or whole books. Readers contribute language, general information, familiarity with standard sentence structure, and acquaintance with such linguistic ornaments as description, comparison, categorization, simile, metaphor, and analogy. Without resonance from the reader, the words convey no message. Without ingenuity and clarity on the part of the writer, fickle readers drift away. When written words and readers' appetites join together, they create participation.

Ironically, the more readers *already* know, the wider and deeper will be their capacities for learning and enjoyment. For example, I recently attended Swingin' with Duke, a concert of Duke Ellington music played by the Lincoln Center Jazz Orchestra with Wynton Marsalis. I have been a music lover all my life. I play the piano (poorly), have an average singing voice, have performed in Gilbert and Sullivan groups, was a member of the church choir for thirty years, subscribe to the Metropolitan

Opera, and love to dance. But I know very little about jazz, improvisation, and swing.

Although the concert was a treat, much of it was beyond me. I caught the melodies and got the rhythms, but I didn't understand the musical jokes, ornamentations, riffs, subtleties, and the genius playing out in front of me. So I had a lovely time, but I understood only what was on the surface. I didn't have the comprehension skills that come with more educated ears.

The same is true with reading comprehension: exposure, experience, and explanation all deepen enjoyment, while creating participation.

Goals

Our goal is to prepare your child for active participation, coaching her in the obvious and subtle aspects of comprehension.

To do this, you must give your child showcases for demonstrating her reading skills, providing feedback as immediately as possible. In particular, reading and writing reinforce each other reciprocally: "To understand it, try to write it."

You also need to entice your child into many different genres of reading, soaking her in various styles and types of expression, widening her repertoires, expanding her exposure, and refining her capacity for analysis. Without such guidance, your child will be able to tap her feet in time to the music, and perhaps remember or recognize a melody or two, but she will neither understand the musical intricacies of the language she meets nor be able to compose or perform in an interesting or entertaining fashion.

Although the categories of factual/accuracy, survey/text, and aesthetic/imaginative blur and blend as we move along the progression of this book, we will still use them, begging the reader's indulgence.

Tools

Tools for Factual/Accuracy Reading Comprehension

Source Sorting. Our language derives mainly from Old English, Greek, and Latin. And although English is reputedly irregular, it is actually 85 percent regular. The irregular words, stumpers to spell and impossible to sound out, come from Celtic. Some examples are *could, are, the,* and *though.* Chances are that a word that "doesn't make sense," a stumper, came down from the Old English created by the Angles, Saxons, Jutes, and Celts.

Many of the words in our language, particularly the vocabularies of medicine and science, are from Greek. When we see a word in which *ch* is pronounced *k,* as in *school* or *psychology,* we can safely designate it as a Greek derivative.

The bulk of our workaday words are from Latin: roots and affixes.

With a slight knowledge of Latin, a mind-set for enjoying puzzles, and a spirit of adventure, you and your child can be language sleuths. Many young readers and writers don't know that words have origins and can be related to one another, just as they themselves are related to the cousins who come for Thanksgiving dinner. Such children fear that every long, new word is the cumbersome invention of a cruel teacher (or textbook writer) and designed to interfere with chances to play video games. When your child discovers how to take words apart, recombine them, or invent new ones, the world of words becomes a giant set of linguistic Legos!

Together with your child, create a poster or scrapbook and divide it into three sections: Old English (or Stumpers), Greek, and Latin. Help your child sort and write in the appropriate section the vocabulary he has met in his subject matter at school or come across in his pleasure reading. Your child will probably delight in strutting his knowledge for family and friends. "By the way, Dad, do you know how to distinguish Old English, Greek, and Latin words? No? Well, don't worry. I can help you."

Beginning even as early as first grade, your child will enjoy being in on the secret of what words actually mean. For example, he can probably figure out why a one-wheel cycle is called a *unicycle,* why a two-wheeler is a *bicycle,* and a three-wheeler is a *tricycle.* With this knowledge in place, ask your child to brainstorm other words with *uni* (see if he comes up with *uniform, unit, or United States*). Can he find other instances of *bi* and *tri*? Of course, older children enjoy this, too. My point is simply that first graders aren't too young to get in on the fun.

The Diseases of the Week. Often, glossaries, particularly in history and science books, list words alphabetically. A more instructive way to organize would be to group by root or by affix, so readers can see immediately which are related, how, and why.

I watched a science teacher teaching children about their bodies. In a segment on problems and illnesses, she told her students that the suffix *itis* means *inflammation.* She asked them to tell her any *itis* they knew of. In a twinkling, they offered *tonsillitis, appendicitis, arthritis,* and so on. They all knew about tonsils, and having clapped the syllables, could easily spell *tonsillitis.* They all knew about an appendix, and several made the connection between the word, their anatomy, and the resource section at the end of a book. One student's grandmother had problems in her joints (her *arths*), and now the student understood the word *arthritis,* could spell it easily and correctly (skillfully avoiding *arthuritus*), and would always recognize and understand it in reading.

For homework on night number one, the teacher asked the students to regroup the words on the vocabulary list, arranging them by affixes. For homework on night number two, she asked them to invent three new diseases ending in *itis*. They brought in *homeworkitis, siblingitis, asparagusitis,* and *liveritis.*

Try this activity with your child, perhaps starting with the suffix *ology,* then moving on to different word roots or affixes for more practice.

Word Detectives. A fourth-grade teacher asked each of her students to come up to the board and write their favorite kind of book to read. The group produced the predictable crop: mystery, adventure, animal, biography, humor, folk tales. Then, Jamil took his turn. He wrote "manyouwill."

The teacher said, "No, Jamil, I asked you to write your favorite kind of book to read."

"I did," Jamil answered.

"That doesn't look like a kind of book to me," the teacher said.

"Well, it is. It's what I like to read," he said, trying to stay sure of his ground.

"Please tell me and the class what it is you have written," asked the teacher.

"Manyouwill," Jamil said, by now close to tears. "You know—it's a book that tells you how to use a machine or something. You read the book and learn what it says, and then, *Man! You will* be able to use the equipment."

The class burst into laughter. Mockery hurts.

Jamil could have avoided humiliation if he and his classmates had known (or learned) that the Latin root for hand is *manus.* From this root they could brainstorm *manuscript, manufacture,* and maybe even produce Jamil's word, *manual.* Once having seen the pattern, they could read, comprehend, and spell it infinitely.

Similarly, a boy in another class wrote, "Last night we went to a good restron."

His teacher asked the class if any of them had ever heard of the word *Taurus.* One said it was her zodiac sign, another that her family has a Ford Taurus. Questioned further, they volunteered that it meant "strong bull." The teacher taught them that the Latin word for thing or things is *res*, adding that the Latin ending *ant* means about or having to do with. She then wrote on the board *res-taur-ant*, showing them that the word restaurant means things having to do with bulls, in other words, a steak house. These fourth graders felt as though they had discovered not only that word, but practically the whole world.

After that, the teacher brought in either a new root, prefix, suffix, or combination every Friday morning, and the whole class played Word Detective. Play Word Detective with your child. Here are some word roots to get you started: *aud, poli, tele, vac.*

True or False. On a piece of paper, develop a list of roots, prefixes, and suffixes, and include the definition. Try to come up with at least five of each. Then give your child a dictionary (*ary*, remember?) and ask her to combine them to make a word that does *not* exist. When she's finished, have her check the dictionary to be sure her new words aren't listed. Then ask your child to define her words and use them in a sentence. One example: *re-circum-able*, meaning something you can go around again. "In England, highway roundabouts are recircumable." Talk about fun! Hello, participation!

New Zoo. This is an activity for all ages. Brainstorm with your child a list of creatures: hippopotamus, spider, monkey, gorilla, cockroach, hornet, rabbit, and so forth. Then, each of you select a creature. Break your creatures' names in half, exchange halves, and recombine the two halves to make a new creature: *spi-key, rab-illa, hor-der, cock-net.* Next, you each draw a picture of your new creature, decide on its habits, and introduce it to the other half. Will the two new creatures get along? Will one be the other's predator? The list of questions is endless.

Have your child write a story about the new creatures. Encourage your child to use onomatopoeia, associating the meaning of a word with its own sound, as in "the *buzzing* of the bees." If this is a noble enough tool for Harvard paleontologist Stephen Jay Gould, for Edward Lear, and Lewis Carroll, it's good enough for schoolchildren. A variation on this is to use names of places: Asia, Africa, Australia, America, Dakota, Nebraska, Springfield, Washington, Seattle. Break them apart, recombine to invent new locations. Write travel brochures. Participate.

Math Word Problems. Here is an eight-step progression for your child to use as she navigates the perils of word problems in math:

1. Preview and mark the math problem using Box It (see page 47).

2. Be sure you understand every single word. Don't skip over such terms as *each* or *area*.

3. Color code all process signs or words that indicate process: green for increase, red for decrease, blue for ratio.

4. Read the problem carefully, usually more than once.

5. Draw a diagram or picture if it helps make the problem clearer.

6. Solve the problem.

7. Write your answer.

8. Work your answer back through the problem to be sure it answers the question(s) in the original situation.

Active, Passive, and Embedded Constructions. An active construction is easy to understand: The girl pushed the boy. (Naughty girl, easy reading.)

A passive construction requires more vigilance: The girl was pushed by the boy. (The girl is on the ground, thanks to the nasty lad.)

Embedded construction confuses imprecise readers: "The boy the girl pushed fell down." Who fell down? "The dog the boy patted seemed sad." Who is sad? "The girl the man saw running went away." Who went away? When your child stumbles on this type of construction, encourage him to visualize, draw the story, or add the word *who* or *whom:* "The boy whom the girl pushed fell down."

A General Suggestion. Many children need to be sitting in a chair and at a table to read accurately. Young readers who slide around on beanbag chairs or loll on their backs, book held high in the air, may look "liberated." However, a closer look reveals that many such children frequently lose their places, skip lines, lose focus, or look out the window. The reader swaying in a hammock may have trouble staying organized in space on the printed page. Body in motion and hammock in motion, eyes may drift or wander. Readers who want to take in information accurately need all the help their bodies can contribute. Provide your child with a comfortable table and chair for reading at home.

Tools for Survey/Text Reading Comprehension

The Five Organizing Questions. Help your child get organized and focused for an assignment by having her ask and answer the five organizing questions before she even opens a book:

1. What do I already know?

2. What do I need to find out?

3. Where will I locate that information?

4. How will I collate that information?

5. What is my end product to be?

With such preparation, your child will sail through the job. On the other hand, if your child leapfrogs this step, she might end up spending time wondering what to do with the information she gathers, unsure which information is relevant, and wondering how to fit the pieces together. Time spent in preparation pays huge dividends of efficiency, comprehension, and participation in reading.

Baseball Cards. Help your child codify and organize the information he is learning in school by fitting it into the format of baseball cards. This requires establishing a grid, slotting information onto it, and keeping everything together in an orderly, portable, efficient fashion, simultaneously creating materials for play as well as study.

For example, let's say your child is studying the explorers in class. Each Explorer Card might include the explorer's name, dates, country of origin, major area of exploration, purpose of exploration, vessels or vehicles used in exploration, major hazards faced in exploration, major helpers or assistants in exploration, and finally a category called Cool Info, an open-ended catch basin for facts that were too interesting to overlook but didn't fit the standard designations.

This format lends itself to periods of history, casts of characters, literary genres, organizations, peoples, places, and things.

Cut and Paste. You can help your child solidify her information and comprehension through cutting and pasting. Here's how.

Let's say your child has been studying our old friend, the impact of the invention of the automobile on American society. Cut index cards into strips, and on each strip ask your child to write something she has studied: a person, place, thing, idea, impact. Put all the slips in a paper bag, shake it up, and ask your child to take ten slips out of the bag, put them in order of importance or sequence, write a brief essay describing what was on the slips, and then show how she wove the ideas or facts together.

Tools for Aesthetic/Imaginative Reading Comprehension

As the World Turns. Human beings love suspense. Pick a story to read aloud—ten minutes a day, if possible; failing that, three times a week or once a week—and then stop at a tantalizing moment. You and your child will listen, laugh, shudder, squeal together, or cry together, knitting a tight emotional bond. You'll discuss the story, know the characters intimately, and be touched in your hearts and minds.

If you are unsure of which story to choose, you might ask a librarian. The search should be for high literary quality, not slick entertainment. One suggestion. There is a translation of *The Odyssey*, by Robert Fagles. The language is superb, and although all of us know parts of the entire story, listeners find suspense as well as familiarity, and the segments fit nicely in ten-minute readings. This would be highly suitable for fourth grade and above. Younger children would enjoy paraphrases but might be overwhelmed by the actual text. It is also on audiocassette.

The Figure in the Carpet. Discovering patterns that link stories together—within or across genres—is one of the exhilarations of being a participating reader. It is the hunt for what Henry James called "the figure in the carpet." No child is too young to begin.

From pre-reading to senior citizens' book clubs, readers can talk about ways in which Richard Scarry books are alike—or how many stories feature space vehicles, or steam shovels, or children left out of birthday parties, or people being happy, or instances of love, jealousy, betrayal, steadfastness, loyalty, or "happily ever after."

Here's a specific pattern search that your child will enjoy (third grade and above).

Start by asking your child to analyze a familiar fairy tale. Let's take *Snow White*. Ask your child who is the main character, what is the problem in the story, who is the evil-doer, who are the helpers, what is the confrontation, and what is the resolution?

Snow White is the innocent heroine, the stepmother is the evildoer, the problem is the stepmother's jealousy of Snow

White's beauty. The confrontations involve the stepmother's attempts to have Snow White killed, including the huntsman who couldn't bear to remove Snow White's heart, and the fateful poisonous apple. The helpers are the dwarves. And we all know what happens at the end, when the prince finds Snow White in the glass coffin. Playing with these elements in a very familiar story sets the stage for further exploration.

Next, ask your child to read *Cinderella,* or read it together, looking for similarities and differences in the two stories. He will probably see quite quickly that both heroines are innocent and motherless, hounded by wicked stepmothers, and that help or rescue comes from small, seemingly powerless creatures.

Once your child is familiar with these patterns, you can move on to less familiar stories. Do the patterns hold up? You might try *Cinderlad, The Twelve Dancing Princesses, The Wizard of Oz,* or *Star Wars.* The hunt is on. Connections emerge. Ideas pop like popcorn.

If your child is accustomed to recognizing patterns, he will have both an extra tool for comprehension, and an extra delight in the hunt.

Landmines

For participation, your child needs:

1. emotional comfort with reading
2. willingness to be playful
3. skills and balance to cross the high wire

1. Emotional comfort with reading. Pay attention to whether or not your child is frightened by the prospect of jumping into reading; if he is, provide reading selections that match his developmental and mechanical levels.

Recently, I was asked to speak at a K-12 school. In deciding on the topic, the principal said to me, "Emotion? Yes, that's important for little children. The primary teachers would enjoy that, but the upper school should hear about testing."

Emotional issues don't end with grammar school. Adolescents have deep needs for emotional grounding. To assume they are beyond this because they are tall, have sophisticated vocabularies, and wear enormous shoes is to deny them their humanity—and to deny the complexity of our world.

2. Willingness to be playful. Ironically, playfulness requires practice. Kids need permission. Adults need to remember that some of the world's greatest insights are products of the playful aspects of serious minds.

3. Skills and balance to cross the high wire. In addition, people who listen a lot but are not thoughtful readers hear words they think they understand. When people (of any age) haven't learned where words come from, they are prone to ludicrous written (and spoken) errors.

See what a teacher, prescribing help for a student with memory weaknesses, wrote, "We are going to try to help Emily use some *pneumonic* devices." Some pump-up!

A student, in a college application essay for a highly competitive institution, described the problems of a Greek hero: "He suffered from an *edible* complex." When's lunch?

VAIL

V: Visualize. From *res-taur-ant,* to embedded constructions about the nasty lad, to finding the figure in the carpet, if your child visualizes, she is a participant in the truest sense of the word.

A: Anticipate. From thinking about an animal in a new zoo, to organizing slips of paper about the impact of the automobile, to having a hunch about the witch, when your child anticipates, he is an active participant.

I: Interpret. From recognizing word origins, to devising a grid for baseball cards, to understanding the vocabulary of revenge, if your child is an interpreting reader, she participates in the feast of reading.

L: Listen. If your child is accustomed to hearing stories that are read aloud, he will develop an ear for the music of language. Like the jazz enthusiasts at the Duke Ellington concert I described earlier, he will absorb nuance and subtlety.

Evidence

This quote is from *The New York Times,* May 4, 1999:

> *"Managed health care has produced new demands on doctors far removed from healing."*

CHAPTER 6

INTUITION

At Promise/At Risk

Playing on the proverb, we could say, Familiarity breeds attempt. Powerful readers have solid skills in phonics and word recognition, analyze word derivations, use punctuation for phrasing, analyze plot, and resonate to genres. In short, they use the strategies that make up the earlier part of this book. In addition, they use intuition.

Intuition? In a book that keeps stressing the importance of accuracy? Yes. Most adults read intuitively. In starting a new book, for example, we probably go slowly initially, gathering speed, power, and enjoyment as we "get into" the story.

"Getting into" the story means becoming accustomed to the names of the characters, the names of the places, the mood of the setting. If it's a desert, we learn to expect words about sand, wind, barrenness, and beauty. If the setting is the coast of Labrador, we anticipate the vocabulary of dampness, fog, storms, fishing, boats, isolation.

We "get into" the writer's rhythms and cadences, sensing

when description is imminent or accustoming our eyes to the spatial arrangement of dialogue. We make friends with the writer, and soon we are moving smartly along, in the manner of having a satisfying conversation with an intelligent friend.

The richer the vocabulary we have inside ourselves, the quicker we are to supply from within ourselves the words the writer is probably just about to use. The deeper and wider our supply of general information, the likelier we are to reach into our mental file folders, pulling up knowledge about deserts or rocky, desolate, and beautiful coastlines. Our own vocabulary and knowledge allow us to intuit the writer's direction.

The fancy term for this process is *anticipatory schemata.* A more poetic term is *casting a linguistic shadow.* Here's how it worked—and didn't work—with two fourth-grade girls, Nancy and Courtney.

Nancy was an orderly, rather stolid little thinker, a marcher and a plodder rather than a vaulter and a leaper. By contrast, Courtney was what we call a "quick and dirty" reader. Although frequently inaccurate, she was buoyed along by a story line like a cork on a current. Skipping and leapfrogging, she ignored what she thought might be boring and got to the good stuff right away.

To accommodate scheduling demands, these two girls came to me together for help with their reading. My conflicting goals were to carbonate Nancy and restrain Courtney. On this particular day, we were reading a story about two explorers in a jungle where danger lurked behind each giant leaf.

Nancy read, "Quit there is a hung. Elephant wait for my single."

Courtney exploded in impatience. "No, Nancy, how can you read it that way? Don't you get it?" Dramatically, she read, "Quiet! There's a huge elephant." Dropping her voice to a whisper, she continued, "Wait for my signal."

Goals

Your aim is to spark intuition, all the while enfolding the skills mentioned earlier. You must help your child enjoy her linguistic hunches, while teaching her to check her accuracy. Striving to bolster language development and fostering understanding of what words really mean, we must also acknowledge the speed with which a competent reader recognizes, analyzes, uses, and combines words. Joining all these elements automatically only happens with teaching, practice, and exercise.

Tools

Tools for Factual/Accuracy Reading Comprehension

Moon Food. We will use onomatopoeia and nonsense again. On a piece of paper, create a chart that says:

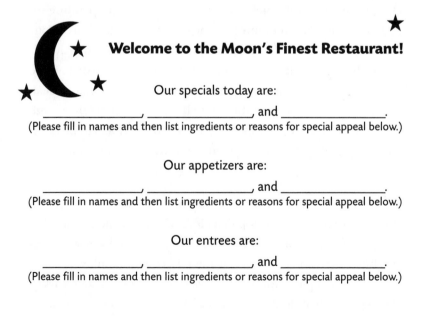

★

★ **Welcome to the Moon's Finest Restaurant!**

★ ★

Our specials today are:

_____, _____, and _____.
(Please fill in names and then list ingredients or reasons for special appeal below.)

Our appetizers are:

_____, _____, and _____.
(Please fill in names and then list ingredients or reasons for special appeal below.)

Our entrees are:

_____, _____, and _____.
(Please fill in names and then list ingredients or reasons for special appeal below.)

SEIZE THE MEANING!

Our side dishes are:

_____, _____, and _____.

(Please fill in names and then list ingredients or reasons for special appeal below.)

Our desserts are:

_____, _____, and _____.

(Please fill in names and then list ingredients or reasons for special appeal below.)

Our beverages are:

_____, _____, and _____.

(Please fill in names and then list ingredients or reasons for special appeal below.)

It is our pleasure to serve you. Please be generous with your tip.
American money accepted.

Once you've made the chart with your child, cut index cards into strips and on each strip write a nonsense syllable, at whatever level of sophistication your child can manage comfortably. Together, put the strips of nonsense syllables in a paper bag. Then have your child pick two or three syllables (depending on proficiency level), combining them into a nonsense word. Your child reads the word, "tastes" its sounds, decides whether it sounds like an appetizer or an entrée, and writes the word on the appropriate blank, including its ingredients and special appeal. Repeat the above steps until your child has a complete menu, and then he can invite you and other family members to place an order! Illustrations are welcome. Appetites soar. Laughter abounds.

Origins. Continue the Source Sorting introduced in chapter 5 with this extension. At the top of a piece of paper, write the heading "Origins" and ask your child to contribute any word whose origins she thinks she can detect, or any new word she doesn't yet understand. For example, a fourth-grade class was reading about Turkey. This brought them to the word *infidel*. Up it went on the poster.

One reader volunteered, "*In* means *not.*"

Another said, "In December we sing 'Adeste Fidilis (O Come All Ye Faithful).' I bet *fidel* means *faith,* so an infidel would be someone without faith."

"But," said another, "*faith* or *faithful* doesn't mean the same thing to everybody." The discussion was lively, the infidel embraced, and comprehension nourished.

Another day, the group was reading about an explorer and ran into the word *circumnavigated.* One boy shot up out of his chair, triumphantly proclaiming, "I can read that! I can even spell it. Watch this!" This kind of joy and power is rocket fuel to intuition and comprehension.

You can also apply this same strategy at home to sports (e.g., *triathlon*), anatomy (e.g., *arthritis,* as we saw earlier), science (e.g., *geography, geology*), the calendar (e.g., *January* or *October*), and to virtually every discipline in a curriculum. All it takes is your alertness to the possibilities—and a little knowledge—to get launched.

You're Kidding. In Gilbert and Sullivan's *Yeomen of the Guard,* Jack Point, the family fool, sings,

> *I can teach you with a quip if I've a mind,*
> *I can trick you into learning with a laugh.*
> *Oh, winnow all my folly, folly, folly,*
> *and you'll find a grain or two of truth among the chaff.*
> *When they're offered to the world in merry guise,*
> *unpleasant truths are swallowed with a will.*
> *Oh, he who'd make his fellow, fellow, fellow creatures wise,*
> *Should always gild the philosophic pill.*

Amelia Bedelia and *The King Who Rained* are gold mines. Together with your child, read a few sections from one of these books, being sure that he gets the jokes, and then ask him to make up his own.

The advice columns *Dear Abby* and *Heloise* lend themselves magnificently to parody. One second grader wrote:

Dear Heloise,
Last week when my family went on a picnic, I got ants in my sand-
wich. I didn't see them, so I ate half of it. Then my sister told me it
was full of ants, so I screamed and spat it out. Now I have dead ant
spots on my favorite shirt. What should I do?
Spotted in Spokane

Dear Spotted in Spokane,
Don't be upset. Simply make some ant-i spot cream. Combine some
saliva, your mother's shampoo, and several spoonfuls of vinegar.
Scrub it onto the spots briskly with your sister's toothbrush. Then
run for your life.
Heloise

Definitions. As mentioned above, accuracy and intuition are symbiotic. In contrast to wild guesses, productive intuition is an informed leap, resting on understanding of the overall topic or issue. This, in turn, requires precise understanding of subsidiary concepts and vocabulary. This, in its own turn, means accurate interpretation and definition of terminology.

To define a word, the speaker or writer must grasp and describe its salient feature, at the same time connecting it with the salient feature of its overall category. For example, if I said, "I am thinking of something that might be yellow or blue, that probably has springs, and that most dwellings have," no one would know what I was talking about. I haven't been specific enough. On the other hand, if I said that a sofa is a piece of furniture, sometimes upholstered, which is used for sitting or lying, and which can accommodate more than one person, I have given solid, specific, and sufficient information.

The ability to define is intimately connected with the ability to summarize, a vital comprehension (and thinking) skill. Many children have not learned to make succinct definitions: They ramble, littering their explanations with scraps of peripheral information, but never hit the bull's-eye. They need practice. Here's a way to practice with your child.

Explaining that the ability to define is a foundation of clear thinking—and is related to the ability to summarize—start by naming a common tangible object, and then ask your child to identify its overall category. Once that is agreed upon, ask her to say precisely how the object fits in the category and how it is the same as and different from other objects in the category. Then write the definition on a piece of paper, asking if there are any extraneous details, and whether there are enough specifics. Together, you and your child can practice defining familiar, tangible objects until she is comfortable with the process and the product.

Then, it is time to move to more abstract words: emotions, remote objects, places, people, and things.

If your child can define crisply, she can file ideas efficiently, and thus retrieve them readily to use them powerfully.

Tools for Survey/Text Reading Comprehension

How to Meet a Book. Show your child how to make the acquaintance of the book or material he is about to read. Here are six steps you can pass along to your child:

Meet Your Book

Step One. Read the title of the book, as well as the titles of the chapters, if any. Think about what the individual words mean and what they mean in combination. Is there any discrepancy, twist, or word play? For example, the title of the introduction to this book is a play on words: "Reading for Meaning—The Meaning of Reading."

Your child will develop a perspective on the book by mulling over the writer's choices. And here's a secret from the world of authors: Frequently a writer needs to choose a title before being able to organize the content of the book, yet may have a hard time catching a good title. If the writer pays that much attention, so should the reader.

Step Two. Peruse the table of contents. Note whether it is laid out in chapters or in segments and sections. How many? How long are they? Will each one be readily digestible, or is each one like a small book in itself?

Step Three. Flip through the pages. Are they dense with prose, or airy with dialogue? Are there bullets, lists, outlines, and graphs—or just words?

Step Four. Open the book at random. Read a paragraph. Do the words flow easily? Does the writer move the reader along with verbs and clear nouns, or is the pace weighted down in vague, verbose, passive constructions:

> *It is to be thought that, in all likelihood, reasons for the apparent unmitigated antagonism between these siblings emerge from the affectionate but misguided attentions given to these two by their maternal parent.*

Help. I feel as if I'm walking through thick mud in iron shoes. Tell me instead that two brothers loathe each other because their mother played favorites.

Better still, show me.

> *Selma gave one son a red fire engine for Christmas and gave the other a pair of brown socks, kindling an antagonism that later exploded in murder.*

Choose accordingly. A reader stuck with an assignment in sludge can only pray for endurance.

Step Five. Read about the author, either on the book jacket or inside the cover. What else has the writer written? Do the titles cluster in a genre, or is there a sprinkling of travel, mystery, history? Does the writer seem credible? Lively? Scholarly? Humorous? Solemn? Does the writer's way seem a likely match for the reader's interest or need?

Step Six. If book and reader seem compatible, give it a try. If author and reader don't get along, try a different book. Readers need not finish every book they start.

Who Says? Inference is a major component of comprehension, particularly that which requires intuition. Yet many bright children are unpracticed in reading between the lines. You can show your child how. The best way to begin is with very short paragraphs or stories, followed by three or four questions, which can or cannot be answered from the text. Here's an example:

> The McCall family enjoys living in their new house, where, finally there is a bedroom for each child. There is even a cozy place for Max's dog bed. The neighborhood is quiet, and other families seem friendly. But the McCalls didn't know there was a local ordinance against sidewalk selling, so they were embarrassed when the police came and told Tommy that their lemonade stand was against the law.

Question 1. Do the McCalls have a dog?
Question 2. Is Tommy an only child?
Question 3. How many children are in the family?
Question 4. Do the McCalls have a garage?

Your child might answer the questions from her own experience, not from the text. Example: "Yes, they have a garage, because houses that sound like that always have garages." Or, "How many children in the family? Lots, because it takes a bunch of kids to make lemonade and set up the stand and sell and everything."

Keep your child returning to the text itself with such questions as, "Which word or words tell you that the McCalls have a dog?" You can easily make up your own passages and questions, or you can ask your child to create some.

Tools for Aesthetic/Imaginary Reading Comprehension

Figures of Speech and Proverbs. When you say, "It is raining cats and dogs," does your child think animals are falling out of the sky? No, but your child might not be so sure about many other common sayings, such as "keep an open mind," "he's pretty hard-hearted," or "keep a sharp eye out." Yet without an understanding of these sayings, he is left to literal interpretation, which drives his comprehension (not to mention his enjoyment) into the basement. Here's a way to help.

Brainstorm with your child and compile a collection of figures of speech. Then talk about what each one means. Next, ask your child to secretly select one figure of speech, and write a short story that embodies the meaning. He should not use the actual words, just imply them through the narrative.

When your child is finished, ask him to read his story aloud, while you try to figure out which figure of speech he was using.

This same method works equally well with proverbs.

Both proverbs and figures of speech are short ways of transmitting complex messages, thus they meld well with our earlier exploration of summary and definition.

Story Starters. You and your child each come up with five intriguing story starters, encouraging a wide variety of theme and mood:

After the murder was discovered . . .
Underneath the apple blossoms . . .
This is it! Game time . . .

The happiness that flooded through me was like the feeling of warm soup at the end of a cold day . . .

No. Not again! I hurt from laughing so much . . .

Put the ten story starters in a grab bag. Have your child select one from the bag and then write a story.

Writing is a road to recognition. If you want your child to be alert to genres, and to glom on to stories, you should give her myriad opportunities to write. As your child puts her own ideas and words on paper, she will sharpen her ability to understand what other writers are doing.

Simile and Metaphor. First, explain to your child that a simile makes a comparison, and the words *like* and *as* are tip-offs to simile. A metaphor is a statement and is much harder to understand and to create.

For example, "Ellen runs like a deer" is a simile comparing Ellen to a fast-running deer. "Ellen is a deer" is a metaphor. Ellen may be a deer because she is a fast runner, because she has large gentle eyes, or because she freezes in confrontations. But the writer is making a figurative statement about Ellen.

To practice, write a list of semi-similes on a piece of paper:

as smooth as . . .

as tough as . . .

as bright as . . .

Ask your child for the clichéd, or traditional, responses, and then tell him you are going to outlaw those because they are tired from overuse. Now, you and your child will both invent new ones. Each of you must write five similes, none of which may include a clichéd ending.

Read your similes aloud, and then together try to think of three additional possibilities that fit. For example, the simile might be "as gray as old dishtowels." You and your child might come up with something like these:

as gray as a cloud,
as gray as sadness,
as gray as the surface of the lake on a cloudy day.

Then ask your child to choose a simile, use it as a title, and write a story.

Landmines

Children who read orally without inflection are telling us they aren't "casting a linguistic shadow." Hearing a child read aloud is the only way for us to hear how the child is hearing the words. You need to hear your child read short passages aloud—frequently.

This is also how you will know what use your child makes of punctuation. Some readers "stop and drop" their voices at the end of the line, starting up again in chipper falsetto at the left-hand margin of the next line. Here is what happens:

"At the end of . . . "(*stop and drop*)

New falsetto: "the letter she saw the signature it was a big surprise because she . . . "(*stop and drop*)

New falsetto: "thought she would never find out what happened to him are you in there . . . " (*stop and drop*)

New falsetto: "said her mother."

On and on and on, the reader chants meaningless drivel. As mentioned previously, if your child overlooks punctuation, he needs to color code: marking capitals, periods, and commas in traffic light language—red for stop, green for go, and orange for pause or proceed with caution. He needs to mark quotation marks and dialogue text the way drama scripts are marked, underlining the name of the speaker.

VAIL

V: Visualize. The reader accustomed to making imagery would have been incapable of Nancy's error, cited at the start of this chapter. Your child needs to see the *images* of what she is reading, as well as the words themselves.

A: Anticipate. The reader who knows how to meet a book, as described above, has a strong hunch of how the book will go, so that hooking in to the text and rhythm will be virtually effortless.

I: Interpret. A reader unfamiliar with figures of speech, simile, and metaphor is shackled to the ground of concrete word calling, while liberated readers float and soar.

L: Listen. Shakespeare wrote, "If music be the food of love, play on." If you want your child to love what he reads, you must show him how to tune in to the writer's inflections and cadences. Reading aloud helps. So does punctuation as we see above—and below.

Evidence

The following statement can be punctuated in two ways:

"Woman without her man is nothing."

Do you choose:

"Woman, without her man, is nothing."

or

"Woman: without her, man is nothing."

CHAPTER 7

EMANCIPATION

At Promise/At Risk

When Henry David Thoreau was at the height of his powers and a New England intellectual leader of his time, a skeptic challenged him by saying, "Why should I pay attention to what you say? You're just local. You've never gone anywhere."

Thoreau replied, "I have traveled widely—in Concord."

Those who read with comprehension can, like Thoreau, travel widely—in their own metaphoric Concord. Remaining physically in the same location, they are free to journey to far-off lands, through air and space, on or under the seas, and inside their own and others' minds and souls. There could be no greater emancipation than such lifting of limits and expansion of horizons.

Goals

Exploration, explanation, expiation, exhilaration. These are our goals. Following the progression of chapters in this book, your child can voyage widely, delve deeply, jump gracefully, soar joyfully, and skip nimbly through the kingdoms offered by print.

Like all classic heroes and heroines, your child will have slipped past fearsome threshold guardians, discovered secrets, captured treasure. He will return with the boons: He will read with comprehension because he will own the reason for reading, therefore reading with reason.

As if this were not enough, another benefit emerges. There is no greater boost to self-esteem than being able to go anywhere and learn about anything. Once again, wisdom comes from New England.

Another Massachusetts man, Edward M. Hallowell, physician, teacher, author, psychiatrist, faculty member at the Harvard Medical School—and admirer of teachers—was speaking to a group of educators about preparing students for lifelong learning.

He said, "Remember that time of life, that state of mind, when you were lord of all the fields and king or queen of all the stars, and feel now how much your will to love and dream and risk and create depends on your having had that once, that time when everything was new and possible—and impossible—all at once."

Tools

Tools for Factual/Accuracy Reading Comprehension

Lexicards. Together, through conversation, you and your child should create a list or chart of words pertaining to what your child is studying in school. Write them on a piece of notebook paper and have your child keep it in her binder. We have seen some examples in earlier chapters. For this example, let's say the topic is geography. The burgeoning list might grow to include: *bay, inlet, gulf, sea, ocean,* and even *archipelago, canal,* *isthmus, barrier island, continent.* You might be surprised by how much your child enjoys rolling big words around on her tongue. But she must have practice in: 1) pronunciation, 2) meaning, 3) word derivation and/or spelling.

It is silly and cruel to expect your child to enjoy words that frustrate or humiliate her. Therefore, after deciding that a particular word deserves a place on the chart, there should be pronunciation practice time. How? You guessed it: syllables. First you say the word quickly, then say it again slowly, one syllable at a time, while your child counts. Next, practice saying it together in that way. Your child can clap the syllables as she speaks them. Then, your child, condensing the word with each repetition, practices saying it as a whole. This practice needs to happen daily; repetition grooves the sounds in the speakers' minds.

As the pronunciation solidifies, define the words one at a time (not more than three at one sitting), illustrating them on a piece of paper. Give your child a pack of index cards, which will become her Lexicards. You should use this big term, explaining the word *lexicon* (*lex* = "words or language") and saying that your child will develop a collection of words for each subject in school.

Then write the three selected words for that day on the piece of paper. Using one index card per word, have your child copy the word, turn the card over and write the definition, and make an illustration. The collection of cards serves first as a quick personal review and second as the material for a great set of customized flashcards.

Have your child use this device for each discipline. Obviously, she will end up with several packs, and you can work through different packs with her on a regular basis. It goes without saying that preparation through pronunciation and speaking is an ideal preliminary to reading.

Readers of earlier chapters will quickly recognize that this is a great chance to sort, file, retrieve, use, and combine. Or to use a swifter mantra, it helps your child "park the old, produce the new."

Lexical Conversion. A lexicon is the collection of particular words that traditionally cluster around a topic. For example, in math we have *numbers* and *equals*, in physics we talk about *incline planes*, in music we talk about *rests, measures*, and *notes*. It is entertaining as well as instructive to note that we use these same words with different meanings outside their academic contexts. We enjoy a particular *number* in a musical comedy, *equals* are voters in a democracy, we *incline* to plumpness, we jet around on *planes*, Victorian ladies take *rests* along with smelling salts, *measures* is a culinary verb or noun, and *notes* are thank-you politesse.

In addition to distinctive lexicons, each discipline or genre has its own appropriate constructions, rhythm, cadence, or music. Directions (good ones) are short and clear: Divide the result into four equal parts. Gossip is whisperingly rhythmic: "And did you know that before they ever even came here, people from their hometown had already decided they were (*select one:* winners, losers, lovers)." Here's a way to help your child play with such distinctions.

Write a noncommittal short story on a piece of paper: The boy met the girl. Together with your child, discuss the lexicons of a fairy tale, an insurance policy, a letter to the editor, a riddle, a scolding, a secret, a newspaper article, a book review, or a lie. Then write the name of each lexicon on a strip of paper and put it in a grab bag. Have your child select one of the strips of paper and, using the selected lexicon, ask him to write an ending to the story you started. When he's done, have him read his story aloud, and see if you can deduce the category from hearing the product.

Mad Libs. You can either buy these ready-made or invent them with your child. In a Mad Lib, your child is asked for a specific type of word: describer, action, color, number, animal, place, thing. You then fill the volunteered word in on a blank in a story. The results can be very funny.

For example, you might ask for and your child might answer:

Action word?

Kissed.

Color?

Purple.

Animal?

Slimy-tongued giraffe.

Place?

Birthday party.

The story might read:

Bobby _____ (action word)

the_____ (color)

_____ (animal)

at the_____ (place).

The result would be:

Bobby kissed the purple slimy-tongued giraffe at the birthday party.

Encourage your child to try a Mad Lib with a friend or group of friends; notice that they get completely different results. Your child will see (while laughing) how many varying results can pop up from a single small stimulus. She is also tickling her own sense of anticipation, which we know from our acronym VAIL, is a foundation of comprehension.

Tools for Survey/Text Reading Comprehension

The ABCs of Genres. The alphabet is an underused tool. See how it opens subliminally understood territories and classifications for your child. Write the alphabet vertically on a piece of paper (probably in two columns). Together with your child, see if you can think of at least one genre per letter. For example:

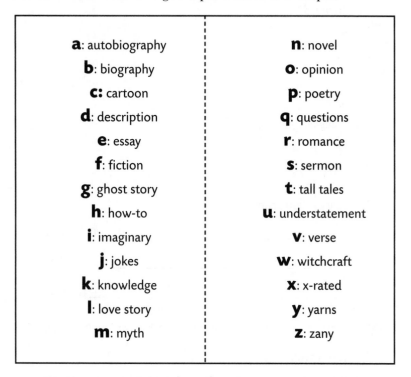

a: autobiography	**n**: novel
b: biography	**o**: opinion
c: cartoon	**p**: poetry
d: description	**q**: questions
e: essay	**r**: romance
f: fiction	**s**: sermon
g: ghost story	**t**: tall tales
h: how-to	**u**: understatement
i: imaginary	**v**: verse
j: jokes	**w**: witchcraft
k: knowledge	**x**: x-rated
l: love story	**y**: yarns
m: myth	**z**: zany

This list, generated by a group of twenty-four students in grades two through five, offers but twenty-six out of a wide field of choices. The point is that you shouldn't have any difficulty in generating items. While your child probably knows the difference between a fairy tale and a scolding, he usually isn't given the chance to label, sort, and categorize the type of reading to which he has been exposed, and with which he is already familiar. Given such opportunities, you'll probably find that your child will make solid and sophisticated connections and observations.

Choose a genre from the list and explore it with your child through reading aloud or having your child read independently, and then asking him to write something in the genre himself.

As we all know from experience, there is no surer way to understanding a topic than to write about it.

Questing. A well-designed question opens up thinking. In contrast to "What was the color of the heroine's dress?" an adult *Gone with the Wind* aficionado might ask, "Why do you think Scarlett O'Hara wore a red 'siren' dress to Melanie Wilkes's birthday party?" This opens up possible discussions of jealousy, revenge, flaunting, and, since it's Melanie, forgiveness. "Why here's our Scarlett. Doesn't she look lovely?"

Applying this to the material with which your child is probably familiar, one might ask, "Who are the winners in *Charlotte's Web*?" "Are they the ones you would have anticipated from the title of the book, or after reading the first chapter?" "In what way do the barnyard and the animals remind you of life at school?"

Some of the six *wh* question words (*who, what, when, where, why, how*) close off further discussion. Others provoke thought. Which are which?

Provocative questions *extend* comprehension as readers retrieve, use, and *combine*.

Tools for Aesthetic/Imaginative Reading Comprehension

The Moon and Her Face. Similar myths and folktales emerge from cultures as different as India and Alaska, telling ageless stories that know no boundaries. Archetypal themes underlie mythic and folktale structure.

When "traveling widely—in Concord," your child may reach back into literary legacy and move forward into original "tea leaf reading tales." Knowing what has come before is a handclasp with history; inventing an extension is to contribute to the future.

You might pursue this line of action by asking your child to read four or five myths or folktales about why the moon changes shape or hides his or her face. In what ways do the reasons differ? How are they the same? In how many instances is the moon "she," and in how many "he"? Why do you suppose this happened? Then, with this cultural foundation, you could ask your child to write a new story of why and how the moon changes.

Of course, there are no right or wrong answers!

Bubble Wrap. The ability to define pins down words. The ability to summarize refines thought. The ability to translate is to make the same idea widely available to different thinkers. You can help your child develop this last capacity, which, obviously, will sharpen her interpretive thinking. The challenge here is to "bubble wrap" a whole story into a small package. The package might be a four- or five-frame cartoon or storyboard, or it might be a four- or five-line piece of doggerel. Here are two examples.

A fourth-grade boy wrote:
Skywalker met
Both Darth and Yoda.
Darth was the action,
And Yoda the coda.

A third-grade girl wrote:
By her mother's grave
Cinderella wept.
Back at the ranch
The ashes she swept.
The sisters were mean
Her stepmother was a witch

But Cindy got to the ball
And ended up rich.

Translation requires understanding. Understanding requires comprehending single words, sentences, paragraphs, and the writer's intention and overall meaning.

Landmines

This is the place to explore the strange phenomenon of strong intelligence and weak scores on standardized tests. Some children have the convenient skill of getting high scores on timed, group-administered, multiple-choice, color-in-the-bubble-with-your-number-two-pencil tests. These children may be brilliant, efficient, or both. Many other bright children, who will go on to great success in later life, bomb on these exercises. In reacting to their scores, we need to ask why.

Some kids hate these tests and race through to escape. Others get nervous when they are timed. Still others are so imaginative that they see possibilities in all the offered answers and can't settle on one. They ruminate and are penalized. Some reflective students enjoy hanging around in each selection and don't finish. A few have spatial confusion and mark the wrong row of bubbles all the way through. And some don't know how to read factual information for accurate response, or how to read bodies of words for salient information. Furthermore, immersion in fantasy is almost never tested on SATs.

In an earlier chapter, we explored specific ways to test comprehension on an individual basis. That is how to find out the depth and strength of your child's skills, as well as the severity and frequency of your child's difficulties. Ironically, standardized tests may reveal the presence of landmines, but sometimes the tests themselves are the landmines.

VAIL

V: Visualize. Without a mental image of Scarlett in the harlot's dress, it would be impossible to understand *Gone with the Wind.* David O. Selznick provided that image for us. You must show your child how to do the same with his own reading.

A: Anticipate. If your child instinctively knows that a verb is waiting to charge onto the scene, she is ready for the action when it occurs. Enough said.

I: Interpret. If your child knows whether he is in farce, fact, or fancy, he can bring the appropriate anticipatory and intuitive skills to the words on the page.

L: Listen. Lexicons have their own music: directions are staccato. Your child needs to listen to the rhythm on the page while she is absorbing the words from the print.

Evidence

Speaking of traveling widely in Concord, how about this notice a highly prestigious school sent home to parents:

"Stuck to the inside walls of the glass display case, your children admired the snails."

CONCLUSION

My favorite college professor used to end his literature lectures with a benediction:

"Good-bye and good reading."

That's what this book is about: *good* reading.

Without comprehension, readers are nomads wandering the pages of print, lanternless and undirected, unguided by landmarks and undelighted by milestones.

The methods and materials suggested here are meant to be compass, maps, and charts, so you and your child can travel on purposeful journeys. From cow paths to turnpikes, roads *do* exist. And whether on village signposts or big green overheads, arrows point to destinations and predict distance.

Each reading journey is different. Some are catch-as-catch-can meanderings, impulsive or sensuous. Many need superhighways. A handful require burrowing through underground labyrinths, searching catacombs for information; and an occasional few are spelunker specials: slow stomach crawling with headlamps to spot an opening or a gem. Others may be a form of hang gliding. Treasured ones are like a long walk on an empty beach with a beloved companion.

SEIZE THE MEANING!

As we find Introduction to the problem, Definition of our challenge, materials for our Foundation, detective skills for Evaluation, light touch and serious purpose for Instruction, energy for Participation, wellsprings for Intuition, and roots and wings for Emancipation, may we all find our combined journeys fruitful, frequent, and varied.

Good-bye and good reading.

DOLCH SIGHT WORD LIST

Created by the late Edward Dolch of the University of Chicago, these 220 words are frequently seen in children's books and in everyday reading. They are called sight words because many of them cannot be learned through phonics or the use of pictures, and therefore must be recognized upon seeing them.

The words are presented in a random sequence instead of alphabetically because the purpose of using this word list with your child is true recognition, not memorization of sequence.

been	could	found	now	yellow
about	ran	big	gave	were
give	well	this	no	which
know	not	put	it	those
because	am	me	live	these
he	came	will	help	to
be	one	old	have	went
may	thank	keep	some	better
when	like	tell	every	them
new	go	has	with	or
my	sit	said	wash	that

SEIZE THE MEANING!

open	can	must	call	jump
myself	your	three	got	best
long	him	pretty	far	grow
its	cold	ask	just	all
how	before	as	she	so
much	would	ride	both	five
I	only	here	by	write
and	is	green	want	make
again	ate	first	read	soon
a	seven	think	once	out
down	fall	red	work	fast
pull	eat	what	walk	blue
fly	see	round	use	from
please	brown	drink	always	if
hot	they	pick	was	after
six	light	today	many	under
shall	sing	draw	saw	but
going	black	own	for	her
off	hurt	made	are	around
ten	come	why	never	show
done	get	over	look	wish
run	good	had	kind	does
white	us	up	there	don't
stop	goes	take	two	at
in	our	sleep	too	who
clean	on	buy	do	did
upon	then	full	yes	play
his	warm	into	an	start
bring	eight	together	laugh	the
say	their	any	hold	right
funny	carry	we	cut	four
were	let	of	very	away
small	find	you	little	try

RESOURCES

Following are some resources that will provide additional information to help you further explore the topics discussed in this book.

---

www.priscillavail.com

Provides information about all of Priscilla L. Vail's books, as well as articles and additional resources on topics discussed in *Seize the Meaning!*

Educators Publishing Service
31 Smith Place
Cambridge, MA 02138

This publisher offers multisensory and organizational materials, originally designed for dyslexics, but which work well for all children. Parents who are eager to find materials that explore word derivations will find them here, along with excellent materials for teaching decoding and encoding.

The International Dyslexia Association
(formerly The Orton Dyslexia Society)
Chester Building, Suite 382
8600 LaSalle Road
Baltimore, MD 21286-2044

This organization brings together physicians, researchers, educators, and parents and offers excellent publications and conferences open to any interested participant.

Modern Learning Press/Programs for Education
Box 167
Rosemont, NJ 08556
1-800-627-5867

This excellent publishing house offers a wide variety of books, classroom materials, videos, and art reproductions for educators and parents. This is a welcome resource.

NOTES

Chapter 1

Humpty Dumpty's words are from Lewis Carroll's *Through the Looking Glass.*

Chapter 3

The chart of phonics elements is from *Recipe for Reading,* by Nina Traub. Thanks to Educators Publishing Service for their kind permission to reprint it here.

Chapter 4

Portions of the opening section, At Promise/At Risk, originally appeared in *Priscilla's Column, The Newsletter of the New York Branch of the International Dyslexia Association,* 1998–99.

The Generalizations section is drawn from Orton-Gillingham training. For more information, consult Educators Publishing Service.

Further suggestions for organization can be found in my books: *Clear & Lively Writing, Words Fail Me,* and *Smart Kids with School Problems.*